STREET GANGS IN AMERICA

STREET GANGS IN AMERICA

BY SANDRA GARDNER
PHOTOGRAPHS BY CARY HERZ

FRANKLIN WATTS
NEW YORK/CHICAGO/LONDON/TORONTO/SYDNEY

ACKNOWLEDGMENTS

I would like to thank Lieutenant Chuck Bradley, head of the Gang Enforcement Teams of the Los Angeles County Sheriff's Department, and his men, and Sergeant Bob Jackson, of the Los Angeles Police Department, for their valuable assistance. Additionally, I would like to thank my friends, Captain Daniel Ruggiero, of the Bergen County Sheriff's Department, New Jersey, and David Bencivengo, for their kind efforts. Finally, I would like to thank my husband, Lewis Gardner, and my agent, Claudia Menza, for their unflagging support.

Library of Congress Cataloging-in-Publication Data

Gardner, Sandra.
Strret gangs in America / by Sandra Garner; photographs by Cary Herz.
p.   cm.
Includes bibliographical references and index.
Summary: Explores the history and current status of youth gangs; how they affect families and neighborhoods; the role of the media; and efforts to end gang violence.
ISBN 0-531-11037-0
1. Gangs—United States—Juvenile literature.   [1. Gangs.]
I. Herz, Cary, ill.   II. Title.
HV6439.U5G38   1992
364.1'06'60973—dc20   92-16618 CIP AC

CONTENTS

STREET GANGS IN AMERICA

INTRODUCTION

At the Los Angeles County Sheriff's Department the list of names, weapons, and gang affiliations tells a grim story: gang-related homicides in 1990 from January through June: almost 600; average age of victim: 21.[1] That is double the number of gang-related killings for the same period in 1989.

There are 90,000 youth gang members in Los Angeles County alone.[2] But gangs are not just a Los Angeles phenomenon. Youth gangs exist all over the country. Their members are younger and older than those in the past, since young people join at an earlier age and remain in gangs until well past adolescence. Sometimes drug deals escalate the level of violence. One of the most current and frightening elements is the drive-by: gangs spraying bullets from speeding cars at their rivals, or at those whom they perceive to be their rivals. A very disturbing aspect of this is that innocent bystanders can get hurt or killed.

Over half a century after Chicago's fabled prohibition gangster shootouts, that city had over 300 drive-by shootings from June 1989 to May 1990.[3] By the end of

November 1990, gang-related deaths in Boston had reached 133 for the year.[4]

In Omaha, police have identified 125 hard-core gang members and 475 wannabes.[5] More than 3,200 active and hard-core members have been identified in Denver.[6] Minneapolis has 3,300; about 30 percent of these are hard-core.[7]

New ethnic gangs have been making headlines recently. Jamaican drug-dealing gangs have been found all over the country, even in small towns like Martinsburg, West Virginia. In New York a new type of "Vietnam War" is being waged—between Vietnamese gang members and their Chinese rivals.

In this book we will explore the history of youth gangs and their current status. We will examine the ways in which gangs have changed, what youth gang members think, how gangs affect families and neighborhoods, and the role of the media in the youth gang problem.

Finally we will discuss the efforts of parents, teachers, community workers, police, and even gang members themselves in helping to end gang violence.

1
LIFE IN GANGLAND

In southern California, a land of year-round blooming greenery, in pastel houses nestled in rolling hills, the young people grow twisted and die quickly. Here in these barrios (neighborhoods) of poverty, Chicano gangs, one of the most prevalent types in the Southwest, flourish. In this chapter, we will look at a Chicano gang, one type of traditional youth gang.

Life here has been affected by gangs for decades—generations, even. Fathers, uncles, and grandfathers have been "soldiers" for the barrio gang. There is even a name for the old-timers: veteranos, the thirty-, forty-, and fifty-year-old members of the gang.

The younger ones are taught by the older members before taking their place as soldiers on this senseless battlefield. They, in time, will teach still younger ones.

This is all they know. This is what they have learned. This is what their parents' lives were and what their children's lives will probably be.

"That's the way it is," says sixteen-year-old Marcos.[1] He looks like any teenager you would see anywhere—except for his eyes. They are constantly darting, scouring the area for danger from enemies, rival gang members who don't even know their victims' real names but only the name of a neighborhood they have sworn to hate.

Marcos is a member of Compton Barrios Largo 36. Compton is a tough Chicano and black ghetto in the Los Angeles area. Thirty-six stands for the 3600 block of the street.

The block is southern California-style poor. Junked cars litter the tight spaces between the squat pink and green broken-down dwellings and the tall, flourishing palms.

The Largo gang "watches out" for this neighborhood, say the members of its crew, who range in age from early puberty to nearly thirty years old. There are about sixty-five active members, not counting the "homeboys"—fellow gang members—in jail.

"When they come out, they'll be back with us," says Jaime, twenty-three. Saying he works in a tire shop, he points to a pile of auto debris. All he is doing, he claims, is "just taking care of myself and my homeboys."

Nineteen-year-old Edgar says, "I've been shot, just because they see you in their neighborhood and they just start shooting." Five years ago he was shot in the right leg. "I was in the wrong neighborhood at the wrong time." He shrugs. "I went to the hospital. They took out the bullet and sewed me up. That's it. No big deal."

Marcos has dark hair and eyes and wears a white T-shirt and black pants, the uniform of a barrio gang. He has added an L.A. Raiders cap. His associates sometimes add a personal touch to the outfit: a gold cross, a button, a pin. Some have "Largo" printed on their caps. Others sew the name on their jackets. The basic uniform—T-shirt and black or khaki pants worn low at the waist—stays the same.

The name Largo can be seen scrawled on caps,

jackets, and walls. That name and the gang it stands for have influenced the lives of these young people since early childhood. The gang so pervades life here that even attending school can be life-threatening.

Seventeen-year-old Alex, who sports the beginnings of a beard, says, "When I went to school yesterday, I got jumped [beaten up] by another gang. They went up to me and said, 'Tell me where you're from.' "

Asking and answering the question about one's home address is a direct invitation to violence. Because gangs are turf-oriented, the very fact of living in a particular location is enough reason to be attacked, shot at, or run over by a car. It doesn't matter to the enemies of a gang like Largo if the suspect is guilty of having done violence to the other crew, or if the young person unfortunate enough to live in Largo territory is even a member of the gang. Living there is reason enough—or not living there, as Marcos and his pals' vigilant scouring of their barrio for intruders testifies.

Alex's response in the school yard was reason enough for him to get beaten up. Badly. "When I said, 'Largo Thirty-six,' the other guy sent a man from their gang, and he started hitting me. I started hitting back, but then there were four of them. Then it was four of us from Largo against four Paragons and ten from Compton Trece and some from 155th Street."

In most gangs, the idea is to hype the macho. Being the toughest gang, the ones who can take it even when they're outnumbered, inflates their image of themselves and furthers their reputation.

"That's the only way they come to Largo, when there's more of them than us," Alex maintains, "but we can hang with [hold our own with] all of them gangs."

Says Marcos, "We'll hang in school, maybe for a couple of years. But some of the other gangs know we're up there and might go looking for us. So after a while maybe we don't go to school anymore."

One of the neighboring middle schools was the scene of sprayed bullets recently. A member of one gang, seeking revenge on another gang, went to the school yard and opened fire through the playground fence. Fortunately no one died—that day.

In June 1990 the guests at a high school graduation party in nearby Norwalk weren't so lucky.[2]

Like millions of teenagers all over the country, the graduating seniors were celebrating in a friend's backyard. But in these parts, backyards are borders of rival gang territory. In this case the wall separating two houses marked the boundary between two violent barrio gangs: Chivas and Norwalk. They had been at each other for several years, resulting in over thirty shootings in the one square mile of sidewalk and buildings. The bloodshed at the party occurred over what should have been a relaxing Memorial Day weekend.

But for those gang members who did go to school and their families and friends, the June graduation party was designated by rivals as payback time.

From the dimly lit outdoors into the middle of the music, dancing, eating, and drinking, a voice shouted the name of the rivals. Within minutes unseen hands pulled the triggers of pistols and semiautomatics. The celebrants ran through the dark, screaming and falling.

The toll: one dead, nine critically wounded. Shooters and victims were sixteen, seventeen, eighteen years old.

"It's the fourth gang-related murder in Norwalk in six months," said one law enforcement officer.[3]

In that same square mile, last year's casualty list included a sixteen-year-old boy. He is paralyzed from the waist down now, blind in one eye, and unable to speak. He was run over by gang members driving a truck. His crime? Riding his bike in his neighborhood. A seventeen-year-old neighbor can't walk without crutches now. While he was walking home, a car drove by, and someone yelled out the name of a rival gang and then shot him. Three of his friends were shot last year in much the same circumstances.

About half the victims of gang violence are simply in the wrong place at the wrong time. They are innocent bystanders, like more than two dozen children and adults recently shot at in the streets of New York City.[4] But other victims are a part of the payback cycle themselves. Often it is hard to tell who's who, since barrio and gang are intertwined for so many young people.

"We're a neighborhood," says Jaime. "We're all homies. We take care of our neighborhood."

Marcos considers himself lucky. "Every time they shoot at me, I'm down on the floor outside a car. They'll come by and shoot at me but hardly ever hit me. They shoot at us walking in the street. They come over here, shoot—and leave. They come to see where we'll be kicking back [hanging out]. I'll be catching them in my neighborhood and say, 'What are you doing in my neighborhood?' They start shooting at us and we'll make them get out. Then we'll get them back, throw our sign 'Largo' at them and get them back."

It's always the other guy who starts the violence, in the recounting of an incident. But it has been going on for so long that no one can remember who fired the first round. Actually, in the past, the war was fought with fists and bats and chains, not the heavy artillery of today. And not the cars. Today's gang warfare is conducted from a "low rider" car with its suspension lowered nearly to the ground.

Prison isn't even the end of it, unless a rival gang member pays someone back in jail.

"We've got homies in prison—county, state," says Jaime. "They go away, but they'll be out one of these days. They'll come out and do the same thing."

Like Marcos, who just came out, he says, for stealing cars. Marriage and children don't end it, either.

"Some are older already, they got kids," says Edgar. "But they just come kick back with us. In case something happens, they're right there to help us out."

Male or female doesn't matter here. Only the neighborhood.

"We look out for the girls," says Alex. "And the girls look out for us. In case something happens to us, the girls will go. And in case something happens to them, we'll be there for them."

Though there are few girls' gangs, girls will join the boys' groups. Or, if they live in a gang neighborhood or have a boyfriend in a gang, they will, at times, serve alongside the boys as soldiers and, consequently, as victims in this war zone. In a later chapter, we will discuss female roles in gangs.

In the back of a car the Largo crew is working on, a bunch of homegirls talk rapidly in English spiced with Spanish street language. They're fifteen, sixteen, seventeen, very pretty, heavily made up, and full of life. But, like their male counterparts, they're jaded and they take an I-don't-care attitude toward the future.

Sixteen-year-old Ana has long dark hair and wears a white bow tucked behind her ear. "We're all homegirls," she says. "We don't have a leader."

"Equal opportunity," says seventeen-year-old Grace, who sports a thick mop of curly hair.

How many are in their crew?

"It's a lot," says seventeen-year-old Sandra. "About fifty of us."

What do they do?

They answer as one: "Kick back."

The peer pressure is so strong here that there is a uniform language as well as a dress code and attitude. There is no other identity, nothing else to depend on, except one another.

"You get used to the shooting," says Ana. "Everybody's been shot at."

"The neighborhood we live in, what can you expect?" says Grace. "Everyday where we live, it's like a daily routine."

"Of course you're scared." Ana shrugs. "But you get used to it."

Why are they shot at?

"Because," says seventeen-year-old Elsa, "they think we're from another group."

Who is doing the shooting?

"Hispanics, blacks, it don't matter," says Grace.

"They're color-blind down there, man," Ana says emphatically. "They'll shoot at you. They won't care. If you're down in one neighborhood, that means you're going to be down to be shot."

Anybody dead?

"A lot," says Elsa. "Don't remind me. One of my friends got shot."

At a time when they should be looking toward a future, they know with a solid certainty that they have none. Homeboys, homegirls—many won't live into adulthood. Or they will be widowed, paralyzed, or blinded from gunfire.

"We know we're risking ourselves every time we go out of our house," says Ana.

"It's not because you want to do something bad," says Grace. "All you want to do is kick back."

"You go," says seventeen-year-old Maria. "You kick back, and maybe you get shot at. That's it."

"Otherwise," Ana explains, "you have to just stay inside your house."

Even that isn't any guarantee. Rival gang fights spill over into living rooms and bedrooms. In some neighborhoods people sleep on the floor, driven by the fear of bullets exploding through their windows.

If there is any hope of escape from the dead-end streets, it might be in the terrible knowledge that Marcos has accumulated during the first sixteen years of this life.

"We know we're going to die one of these days. But we die in our neighborhood. I know what's happening to me," he says, his eyes quiet for a moment. "I tell my younger brother—he's thirteen—what's going up with the gang, so he don't join. I tell him, so it won't happen to him."

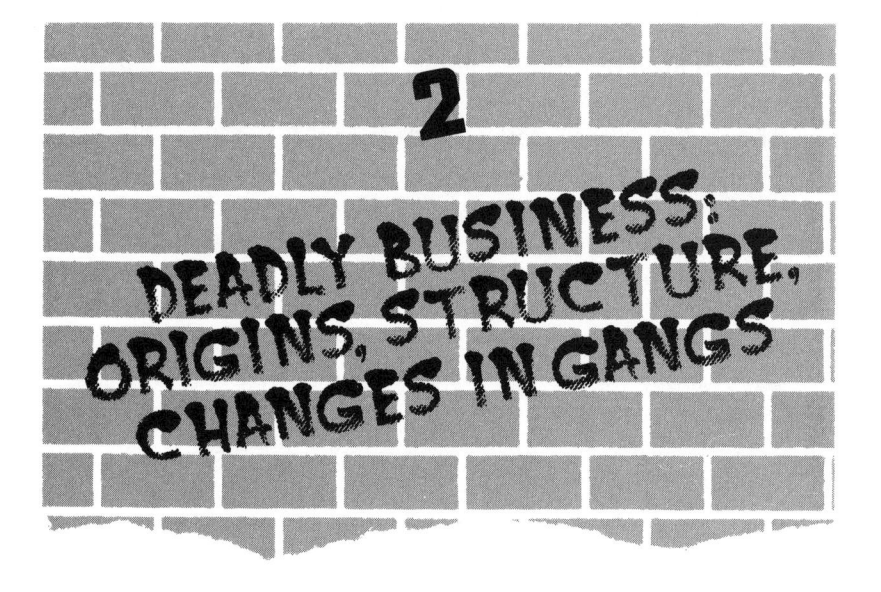

2
DEADLY BUSINESS: ORIGINS, STRUCTURE, CHANGES IN GANGS

Gangs like Largo have been a fact of Los Angeles barrio life for fifty years. But street gangs are not just an L.A. barrio phenomenon. And they are not what they were fifty, twenty-five, or even fifteen years ago.

"It used to be feet and fists," says Lieutenant Chuck Bradley, head of the Los Angeles Sheriff's Gang Enforcement Teams. "Now it's sawed-off shotguns and automatics."[1]

Historically youth gangs have attracted people from poor immigrant families. Most of the young people in the waves of immigrants that crowded into the ethnic ghettos didn't, however, form gangs. Even for those who did, growing up usually meant growing out of and away from the neighborhood corner and, therefore, away from the gang. As adults, they went to work and lived respectable family lives, as their parents had tried to do before them.

Many youth gangs began as groups of inner-city kids clustering together for mutual comfort and support. They would talk and brag, insult one another good-naturedly, and shoot a few baskets in the local school yard.

Around the corner, the adjoining neighborhood had its own group of young people on its sidewalks. Name-calling between the two groups soon led to shoving. Though they didn't start as warring gangs, eventually the neighborhood rivalries escalated into violence. They would fight with punches, kicks, bats, and bricks.

The gangs were both a part of and apart from their neighborhood. The respectable adults who lived there, struggling hard to make a decent life for their families in the new country, disliked and even feared them. The youth gangs, in turn, felt alienated, and strengthened their bonds more fiercely.

Growing up in a ghetto had already alienated these young people from the larger society. They were born in their new country, but they remained outsiders, unconnected to the mainstream. Since these neighborhoods were composed of similar families, the stage was set for the bonding of street gang members who served as an extended family. Because these young people and their families owned few material goods, had little status in society, and had no hope of attaining the American dream, they claimed their neighborhood as their own, for lack of anything else.

The end result was that pride in the neighborhood formed the core of the gang members' existence. The gang and the sidewalk, the streets and houses, schools, parks, and neighborhood stores became the young people's entire identity. That is why asking someone "Where are you from?" came to serve as an immediate means of identifying friend or foe. Identification of neighborhood is how the gang member decides whether to man the barricades or welcome a brother.

GANG CULTURE

Most urban street gangs follow a similar pattern. Their activity rises and falls in cycles as their ranks are periodically decimated by the arrest or murder of numbers of their troops and as new members are recruited from among the younger residents in the neighborhood. Though some gangs have leaders, others do not. And even those with leaders are generally not very well organized. Little thought or planning goes into their activities. Though criminal actions and revenge on rivals are planned to some extent, most actions are carried out on impulse and spearheaded by whoever came up with the idea.

The street gang, thus, has traditionally been an informal group of people who spend time together and get in trouble with the law. In this sense, it is usually an informal peer group rather than a carefully organized racketeering gang. (There are exceptions, which we will note in a later chapter.) A major factor, of course, is that the street gang is committed to violence.

MEMBERSHIP

Traditionally youth gangs have exaggerated the size of their membership to their rivals and the police to inflate their own sense of importance and to intimidate their enemies. These inflated numbers often include both active and affiliate members. Not all members of a gang are equally active. Members generally fall into one of three categories: hard-core members, associates, and wannabes.

Hard-core members have been in the gang for years. Their total identity is wrapped up in the gang. They have few if any interests outside the gang. They have committed crimes, run up against the police, and probably done time in a juvenile detention center or a prison. Most likely the only way they will ever leave the gang is via an extended prison term or a grave. The gang is indeed their life.

Gang associates hang around with the others, but may or may not show up on the particular corner on a regular basis. They will join in the activities and identify themselves to others as members of a gang. Maybe they haven't yet been arrested for major crimes or served time. They haven't killed anyone for the gang's honor or reputation. And they may turn away from the gang life.

Wannabes, like imitators of other groups—rock groups, for example—mimic the mannerisms, dress, language, and customs of that group they "want to be" a member of. Wannabes are usually preadolescents, often as young as eight. They dress up in gang regalia, scribble the gang logo on their schoolbooks, walk and talk like their heroes. Wannabes take on the trappings of the older youths they see around them, but they often have no idea of what gang life really entails. Unfortunately, the neighborhood gangsters are their role models. Because wannabes have not really gotten into gang life, they can get out of it before it's too late.

INITIATION

New members are generally recruited from among younger brothers and neighbors in the area. Though they are usually well known to the group, recruits have to prove their worthiness by undergoing an initiation rite. This is called being "jumped" or "courted" in. The recruit may be invited to drink or use drugs with the gang. The others may beat him up to test his mettle. A prospect may be required to prove himself and his loyalty to the gang by committing a crime—a mugging or an assault, perhaps, or a drive-by shooting. This ensures his loyalty, since he is implicated in the crime.

COLORS

Some gangs, especially in Los Angeles, proudly display their regalia, or "colors." However, if they are worried about identification by police, they disguise their outfits or wear them only on safe occasions around friends.

Colors are a gang's identification. Wearing or "flying" colors is a direct admission of gang membership. The gang will have a particular style of dress, although some gangs dress similarly to others, and the logo may appear on caps, shirts and jackets. The logo often includes the gang's name, location, and symbols of specific acts of violence.

In the 1950s, members of youth gangs wore denim or leather jackets illustrated with elaborate drawings and decorations, like those of the "outlaw" motorcycle gangs, including the Hell's Angels. Now outfits are generally less flashy and follow a uniform dress code, as in the white T-shirts, baggy pants, and baseball caps of Hispanic gangs. Often the only differentiation among these gangs' dress is their logo. Some gangs, however, like the Crips and the Bloods—two black gangs—take on a color of their own: Bloods, red; Crips, blue.

GRAFFITI

Writing graffiti is sometimes called "throwing a placa." Gang logos as graffiti are displayed as a public statement of importance, territorial rights, and intimidation. Graffiti incorporate the symbols of a gang with statements of self-importance, territoriality, and threats to other gangs.

When plotting to wreak havoc or pay back in the ongoing game of revenge, a gang will cross out a rival gang's graffiti and scrawl its own over it. This is a direct incitement to violence. Since the gang's purpose is to build self-esteem and identity through membership in the gang, rubbing out the name is tantamount to rubbing out the gang itself.

Some gangs carve out their turf with graffiti. Turf is the area or territory that a gang claims for its own. It may comprise a few square blocks or a section of a neighborhood or a housing project. These efforts to stake a claim may turn the gang's turf into a giant canvas. Members splatter graffiti over every fence, wall, pole, and building in their neighborhood. Covering an area with graffiti is a statement that the gang has put down roots.

OTHER SYMBOLS

Another form of gang signature is the use of hand signals. Throwing a sign, according to the Largo gang, means using hand signals as a threat or territorial statement to rivals. Hand signals are an up-front direct challenge in a one-on-one or group-to-group assault.

Body tattoos are another method of identification for some gangs. Tattoos can be placed on the arm, the chest, the back—virtually anywhere on the body. Elaborate or simple, the message is the same: the gang ID. Here the gang's logo actually becomes part of the young person's body, a permanent reminder of his commitment to the gang.

One member of a Chicano gang, pulling up his shirt while being searched for weapons by the police, proudly showed off his gang "visuals." Black and red tattoos embellished his body from neck to waist and totally covered both arms. Every bit of skin was adorned with gang markings. That type of total identification with a gang leaves little space for any other life-style.

Black gangs do not have a tradition of gang tattooing. Recently, however, some black gangs and members of ethnically mixed gangs have adopted Latino-gang-style tattoos.

Additional differences between black, Hispanic, Asian, and other ethnic gangs will be discussed in a later chapter.

GANG NAMES

The gang's ID—say, the Eighteenth Street Killers—identifies it as inhabiting Eighteenth Street and enhances its reputation for violence. The members, too, may use a gang ID.

A new recruit may take, or be christened with, a "street" or gang name. That name may reflect the personal attributes of its wearer—for example, Flaco (skinny) or Pee Wee.

Some street names pay tribute to a new member's gang hero or mentor. Little Tony sees himself as a junior version of Tony; Baby Tiny is a younger Tiny. This is another manifestation of the role-modeling aspect of gangs.

Street names supply their owners with a sense of identity and status in the world of violence.

Sergeant Ralph Kemp, who heads the Albuquerque, New Mexico, police gang unit, says, "By changing his name to Mad Dog, he feels that he's somebody."[2]

CHANGES IN GANGS

Youth gangs have always been made up of members of the ethnic groups occupying the lowest rung on the American socioeconomic ladder. Today's gangs are primarily black and Asian, along with those Hispanics living in conditions no better than those of their grandfathers.

But, like their poverty-stricken Irish, Polish, and Italian predecessors, today's youths have choices about how to spend their time, whom to choose for friends, and what sort of future to work toward. Everyone who grows up in a culturally and economically deprived community does not end up as a criminal gang member.

There are a variety of reasons why some young people join and remain with a street gang. Many of the same basic needs that motivated yesterday's youth gang recruits propel young people into gang life today: the need for identity and self-esteem, alienation from society, poor social conditions. But some hard facts of life in today's society have a part in causing teenagers to gravitate toward gangs and in the reasons why gangs have spread and changed for the worse. New, deadly ingredients have been added to the breeding ground for violent gangs, resulting in a dangerous mix exploding in today's world. These new ingredients are a lack of jobs, an increase in poverty, and the proliferation of drugs and violence in our society.

A New York Times article on the rise in youth violence cited a 1989 report by the House Committee on Children, Youth and Families about a "national emergency: of growing violence by and against youth," and added that "most experts agree that the violence reflects a breakdown of families, schools, and other community institutions."[3]

POVERTY

The proportion of young people growing up in poverty has increased dramatically in the last fifteen years. Children under eighteen are now our country's poorest age group.[4]

The U.S. Census Bureau states that 12.6 million Americans under eighteen, or one in every five children in the country, live in a household with an income below the government's poverty line.[5] Two out of every five black and Hispanic children are poor. Representative George Miller, chairman of the House Select Committee on Children, Youth and Families, stated that his committee found that "millions of children are unhealthy, uneducated, and unable to participate in the highly technological economy of the future."[6]

FAMILY STRUCTURE

Senator Daniel Patrick Moynihan, chairman of the Senate Finance Subcommittee on Social Security and Family Policy, stated, "The locus of poverty today is neither regional nor racial. It is the female-headed household. In 1960," he continued, "67 percent of black children lived with two parents; the proportion is now down to 32 percent. The trend is the same for Hispanic and white children."[7]

Years ago poor and immigrant families could work toward a better future. Today, many poor families are plunging downwards with little hope for a decent life for their children.

One result of this is that the families of some young people who gravitate toward gangs are malfunctioning to the point of nonexistence. Even in two-parent households, both parents frequently work long hours at low-paying jobs or are chronically unemployed.

Some young people are living in single-parent homes headed by a parent who is financially and emotionally overwhelmed. Sometimes there is drug or alcohol abuse. Access to good education may have been a problem. This, in turn, may render a parent unable to use those social services and community programs that do exist to cope with multiple family problems. In *Dangerous Society*, a study of Detroit gangs, Dr. Carl S. Taylor says: "When the home fails and the schools, churches, and the social welfare program miss, chances are a scavenger group is being formed." He defines scavenger gangs as loosely organized youth gangs.[8]

In this type of family, young people literally raise themselves, without adult care, guidance, or positive role-modeling. In some instances, teenagers have to bear the responsibility for raising younger siblings when they are still in great need of parenting themselves. And, depending on how severe the parents' emotional disturbances are, the teenagers may be emotionally, physically, or sexually abused.

Another type of family problem develops when parents are non-English-speaking and heavily steeped in the old-country culture. Teenagers are caught in the middle

27

when peer pressure to be an American teenager clashes with the family's traditions and values. This setup ignites stormy conflicts between parent and teenager, as the young people tug and pull and finally shred the fabric of the family relationship at an early age, leaving them ripe for relying on the local surrogate family: the gang.

To further complicate matters, because of their language and traditions, some immigrant families tend to be clannish. Their cultural pride and experience with bigotry may prevent them from asking for help from a society they view as prejudiced, unresponsive, and difficult to understand.

In generational gang families, the entire family—children, parents, and their parents before them—identifies with the neighborhood gang. As with other types of role-modeling, growing up in a gang family almost guarantees firm entrenchment in the gang at an early age. In this situation, the two "families" become nearly indistinguishable. The biological family has totally merged with the neighborhood gang family. This could be compared with a mafioso-style gangster family, in which the family is part of a larger "Family"—the extended family of the criminal gang. Patrolman Mike Schoeben, Minneapolis Police gang specialist, says, "We're seeing generational gang families—whole families in gangs—migrating from Chicago, during the past five to ten years."

VIOLENCE AND SOCIETY

The escalating violence in today's youth gangs mirrors the escalating violence in our society. Increasingly powerful deadly weapons are proliferating wildly and are all too readily accessible. Everyday violence, especially in large cities, has shot up to such extraordinary heights that inhabitants shrug and throw up their hands, accepting it as a fact of life.

A 1990 television special report, "Guns: A Day in

the Death of America," told the story of "all deaths by guns which took place within a twenty-four-hour period on July 16, 1989. When it was over, sixty-one people had been shot dead" in this country. The documentary was a frightening commentary on our violent society: "In one year, handguns killed 8,092 Americans. All across America, inner cities have become war zones. We live in a country at war with itself."[9]

With the increasing availability of guns, these gangs began to play their deadly one-upmanship games for higher stakes. Young gangs are now armed with automatics and shotguns. That fact and the fact that young people remain in street gangs till an older age, due to their feeling locked in to this way of life, has spawned the new form of guerrilla-style gang warfare known as the drive-by shooting—spraying bullets from a speeding car.

MOBILE SOCIETY, DRUGS, AND VIOLENCE

The mobility of our society has a direct impact on the spread of youth gangs. When hard-core gang members move with their families to another city or state, they take their violent street culture with them and transplant it into their new surroundings. This gives them an identity and status in their new neighborhood. This may contribute to the spread of youth gangs in the country.

Even more than our mobile society, drugs are a major element in the spread and increasing violence of youth gangs. With the advent of crack cocaine in the mid-1980s, black gangs, the best known of which are the Bloods and the Crips, grew larger and more violent as their involvement in narcotics grew.

However, according to Sergeant Bob Jackson of the Los Angeles Police Gang Unit, "We don't see entire gangs becoming drug gangs. What we see is individuals becoming involved in the narcotics business. And the more gang members are involved in a narcotics business, the less they function as a street gang. At that point they've moved into organized crime.

"This business enterprise," he says, "does what any business would do: send individuals to other states, to test the market."[10]

Other gangs, particularly Hispanic ones, are not fighting over a corner of the drug market—at least, not yet—though they do use marijuana and sell heroin. "They sell heroin in their own neighborhoods," says Lieutenant Bradley. "It's still a turf war, with the Hispanic gangs."[11]

PEER PRESSURE

Eighteen-year-old Johnnie is graduating from high school and preparing for college in the fall. His next-door neighbor, Martin, spends his days and nights on the streets.

Why? Johnnie has a strong sense of himself and made determined efforts to set himself on the right path for a positive future. Martin, on the other hand, never thought much of himself, though he adopted a macho front to cover up his feelings. His bravado fit right into the local gang culture, and Martin easily slipped into it. The immediate gratification—the instant sense of belonging and identity—was hard to resist.

Professor Irving Spergel, a University of Chicago sociologist who has studied gangs, says that young people join gangs because communities are in transition, families are not providing supervision or affection, schools are not doing their jobs, and few job opportunities are available to teenagers.

"But," he adds, "in the same family, one teenager will join a gang, the other, not. Maybe one is getting his needs met by the family and the other isn't. And there are different kinds of young people."[12]

Resisting peer pressure, as every teenager knows, is tough. You have to have high self-esteem, strong mo-

tivation, and belief in a future. A good support system—
a caring family, respectable role models, and a healthful
environment—play a big part in resisting peer pressure
that is self-destructive.

Teenagers in Chicago's drug- and gang-infested
neighborhoods say that strong family support has helped
them resist peer pressure to join drug-dealing gangs.
Eighteen-year-old Lacrista Ewing says her mother has
given her the values to be able to resist gangs. She hopes
to become a police officer or a teacher. Fourteen-year-
old Ervin Barker would rather shoot baskets than sell cocaine in a gang. His older sisters have warned him about
drugs and gangs.

Unfortunately, many young people growing up don't
have the strong family support to help them fight the
intimidation and peer pressure of youth gangs.

In the next chapter, we will examine how the new
elements—powerful weapons, cars, and escalating violence—have made life in some neighborhoods a terror-
filled existence.

3.
DRIVE-BY AGONY

In a run-down street in Lynwood, a city of working-class black and Hispanic families in the Los Angeles area, Lorna Hawkins is living testimony to the fallout from Long Beach Boulevard a block away. Here, the sounds of gunfire from warring drug gangs are as routine as traffic noises exploding into the once-quiet neighborhood.

Inside her neat, modest home, Mrs. Hawkins, a wiry, energetic woman, tells her story, illustrated by pictures of her murdered son, Joe. Joe was killed at the age of twenty-one, an innocent victim of a drive-by shooting. Photos from infancy to his last year of life cover the piano and tables, along with pictures of the rest of his family: parents, brother, sisters, and a two-year-old son, Joe Van.

"I'll always remember it. It was the night before Thanksgiving on November 23, 1988," Mrs. Hawkins recalled. "It was around eight-thirty. I was tired from cooking. I lay down to rest so I didn't hear Joe come in and go out again. He stopped in on his way home from work before he went to visit his baby son who was three months old. After he left here, he went around the corner to the drugstore to pick up something for the baby. At that moment, four kids in a car drove by and screeched to a halt. They yelled out the name of one of the local Crips gangs, the Pendleton Crips, and started shooting.

"One bullet hit Joe in the neck and severed the artery to his brain. He was dying from that minute. My husband and I drove him to the hospital. A week later we had to ask to disconnect him from the respirator."[1]

Once the worst of her shock and grief had lessened, Mrs. Hawkins grew more and more angry. "He was an innocent bystander, killed on the streets for no reason at all. And we couldn't get any witnesses to testify. They were too scared." She shakes her head.

"We've lived here for twelve years. It used to be a quiet neighborhood. Now it's out of hand. We're squeezed in between the Hispanic and the black gangs," she explains. "The cemeteries around here are full of victims of violence. We're a neighborhood. We shouldn't give it up to a bunch of hoodlums."

Mrs. Hawkins put her energy and anger to work. She decided to wake people up and get them to take back their neighborhoods. She felt that talking about her own terrible experience could help accomplish this by opening up a dialogue.

She made her story the focal point for a talk show and took it to a local cable television station. She called the show "Drive-By Agony." "Because my son was killed in a drive-by shooting. And because I know all the agony it's brought me," she explains.

"Drive-By Agony" features Mrs. Hawkins as the show's host. Her guests on the program include mothers of victims, representatives of law enforcement, elected officials, community members, and positive role models for young people.

Mrs. Hawkins began by obtaining a list of victims' families from the Lynwood Sheriff's Department. At first she had difficulty getting people to come forward and tell their stories on the air. But as the shootings escalated, more and more mothers of victims of violence agreed to participate. Now the program has gathered momentum. And the people who are sick and tired of the senseless violence laying waste their communities are using it as a forum to take their message to their neighborhoods—"to sweep the neighborhood clean," as Mrs. Hawkins puts it.

One of her "drive-by moms," as Mrs. Hawkins calls them, is Fern Stamps, from the neighboring city of Carson. Mrs. Stamps takes her own show on the road to the teenagers in the state's juvenile correctional facilities.

Like Mrs. Hawkins, Mrs. Stamps and her family are victims of neighborhood youth gang violence. Mrs. Stamps's son, Kemani, one of a pair of identical twins, was murdered in January 1988. "It was a random shooting," says Mrs. Stamps. "My son and his brother were taking out the trash. When they went outside, some kids drove by. There were two of them with bandanas over their faces. One of them pulled a gun and shot my son."[2]

Her son was fifteen years old. His killer was sixteen. The fact that the killer was another young person made Mrs. Stamps very angry. "My anger was at the community," Mrs. Stamps explains. "I was angry that this could happen in our community. And," she asks, "what went wrong in this kid's life? Something is seriously wrong when any of our kids feels that in order to establish some self-worth or identity, they have to take somebody's life. It could have been anyone's child. It happened to mine."

Like Mrs. Hawkins, Mrs. Stamps felt that she had to take action. She began her mission while her son was still in the hospital hooked up to a respirator.

Mrs. Stamps took a photograph of her dying fifteen-year-old, alive only because of the machines doing his breathing for him. "I wanted the kids to see him," she explained. "Because watching violence on television has desensitized our children to real violence. And no one talks to the kids about what happens to everyone after the violence occurs."

Since then Mrs. Stamps has devoted herself to the education and rehabilitation of teenage gang members who have committed violent crimes. She travels to the California Youth Authority's juvenile correctional facilities as part of the victims' awareness program on homicide. She tries to make an impact on the youth gang members with her message. And she succeeds.

She talks to teenage gang members serving time in prison for murder as if they were her own children. She tells them about respect for society. She tells them about the consequences of their actions. On others. And on themselves.

She shows them what happens after they commit the crime. She uses two poster-sized photographs of her dead son to drive her point home: one, a school picture of him; the other, her son on the life-support system in the hospital.

She tells them: "This was my child. He was fifteen years old. This school picture was his last picture taken before he was murdered."

She turns to the second photo. "This is Kemani hooked up to a respirator. The gunman shot him in the back of the head. The bullet dragged through his brain and remained lodged in his forehead. If he had lived, he would have been a vegetable," she says.

"When I share my story with these kids," Mrs. Stamps says, "they'll say, 'Why didn't anybody tell me this before I committed the crime?' "

The prison chaplain can tell when Mrs. Stamps has paid a visit. His office will be full the next day.

"They write and tell me they can't sleep," Mrs. Stamps says.

A public service announcement on the "Drive-By Agony" television program features children at home and on a playground. "In my neighborhood, they shoot you for just wearing a color," says a small girl. "They're shooting by my house," says a little boy.

In one elementary school in the area, one hundred parents bought uniforms for their children to wear to school. The parents hoped that the muted colors would prevent their youngsters from being targets of accidental shootings because of the colors favored by local gangs.

Wherever there is violence, especially from gang- or drug-related crimes, gunmen in cars, spraying bullets into crowds and through doors and walls, have become part of the picture. In these neighborhoods, parents pull their young children into the house as soon as the sun fades, issuing warnings about the dangers outside.

It's not just the nighttime that is dangerous, however. Broad daylight can be just as murderous.

One day early in June 1990, gunmen shooting it out in a Los Angeles alley fired in the direction of a yard full of children. A one-year-old baby was hit in the thigh.[3]

That same June, four-year-old Gilbert Perez, Jr., was killed when random shots fired from a car landed in the Perez family's car. His mother had been driving home from a restaurant in Pomona, California.[4]

Other children in southern California have been hit by stray bullets: a three-year-old girl shot in the arm while playing on her porch, a seven-year-old boy shot in the chest.[5] And there were others whose lives ended with a gang bullet: a young girl killed while playing softball in a yard, a small boy murdered while talking to his friends.[6]

Some bullets are sprayed from cars; others are fired by individuals on foot. They are meant for someone else in an argument over drugs or stolen goods. Or they are meant as payback in gang turf wars. Today gang grudges are settled—for the moment until the next round—with bullets. Those who are in the way—on a corner, in a car, in their yard—can end up as victims of stray or random gunfire. This is often referred to as "being in the wrong place at the wrong time" by those who try to explain the reason for the victims of violence.

"Drive-bys in Chicago are very clearly gang-related," says Professor Irving Spergel, of the University of Chicago.[7]

"We also have 'walk-up' shootings," says Patrolman Mike Schoeben, Minneapolis Police Department. "They just walk up and shoot some guy in the head."[8]

Police, as well as mothers like Lorna Hawkins, are tired of the constant refrain of gunfire.

Says a Los Angeles sheriff's deputy: "If it's gunshots, nobody even bothers to call us unless they see somebody down [on the ground, dead or wounded]. It's such a common occurrence every night. We drive there—there's nobody there, nobody saw anything. They get tired of calling us. We get tired of going."[9]

The hospitals are getting tired of treating the victims, too.

Huntington Memorial Hospital in Pasadena gave as its reason for closing its trauma unit that it could not afford to spend any more money treating poor victims of gang violence from south-central Los Angeles, twenty miles south. One surgeon said, "You can't help but be unhappy when you have a patient due for surgery and you have to postpone it to deal with a gunshot victim from south-central."[10]

On the other hand, U.S. Army surgeons are benefiting, in a strange learning experience, from the bloody fallout of Los Angeles gang violence. Because of the sheer volume of warlike wounds inflicted on these victims of automatic and semiautomatic weapons, the U.S. Army is training its surgeons in trauma treatment at the Martin Luther King–Drew Medical Center. This county hospital sees so many gang-violence victims that the surgeons-in-training are learning how to treat real war victims by treating these victims of local battles.

Random or stray bullets also claim victims outside California. In other urban areas, drug- and robbery-related rival feuds have spilled over into neighborhoods, affecting the way of life and the very lives of its residents.

37

Historically, Chicago has been linked with Prohibition gangsters of the 1920s, who used to blast their rivals with tommy guns in restaurants, at barber shops, and on the streets. Now, seventy years later, Chicago streets are the scene of shootouts once again. But this time, the crimes are affecting the lives of the respectable residents of the city and its suburbs.

One of these was Curtis Sims, a mechanic, shot on Chicago's South Side in June 1990 by two men in a car.[11] Police say he was murdered because he wore a baseball cap tilted to the right. The killers were members of a gang that wore their caps tilted to the left.

The irony is that during the same month the headquarters of Chicago's infamous El Rukns criminal street gang was torn down after years of criminal activity. El Rukns began as the Blackstone Rangers, a black youth gang, in the late 1950s. In the 1960s, they were seemingly reborn as a public service group. They finally gained a reputation as a supergang—a gang that was well structured and had a membership of over five hundred.[12] In the 1970s the leaders of the Rangers, who were now adults, formed a group called El Rukn, a Muslim sect—a paramilitary organization, according to the police. In 1989, many of the gang's members were arrested, and bulldozers tore down their headquarters on Chicago's South Side.

Despite the waning of one of the last of the big 1960s gangs, there were 334 drive-by shootings in Chicago between June 1989 and May 1990.[13] Police believe the violence is connected to drug dealing.

"Years ago gang members used to ride on bicycles and have fist fights," said Chief John Townsend of the Chicago Police Detective Bureau. "Now they drive Buicks and Cadillacs and have gunfights with high-priced weapons."[14]

Violence of a brand-new type, the drug- and car-connected drive-bys, was rising in Chicago and in other cities all over the country.

A 1989 report from the Crime Control Institute in Washington, D.C., reported a dramatic increase in bystander deaths in New York, Washington, Boston, and Los Angeles.[15] The study found that the fastest growing category of bystander deaths was "drive-by shootings," in which drug gangs establish their turf by shooting randomly into crowds.

"Your risk is increasingly a matter of being in the wrong place at the wrong time," said Lawrence W. Sherman, a professor of criminology at the University of Maryland. "It's a real innovation in homicide," said Mr. Sherman.[16]

In the next chapter, we will discuss how youth gangs have been changed by the combination of drugs and violence.

4

VIOLENCE
AND DRUGS

"Little Ducc went on his first mission, a drive-by as an observer when he was twelve. Next day he was ready to fire on his own."[1]

Ducc, now fourteen and in juvenile detention, is a member of a Los Angeles Crip gang. The Crips and their chief rivals, the Bloods, black youth gangs, have become nationally known for their drug-dealing and violence.

Though youth gangs have been a fact of urban street life for over a hundred years, their violence has risen to dangerous new heights today. Furthermore, the effects of the violence now extend into the everyday life of major cities.

New, too, is the drug epidemic that serves as the catalyst for some of the gang violence.

Back in the 1970s, gang turf wars were fought over a few blocks of sidewalk or a park. Weapons were less sophisticated. Cars were not readily available, since most gang members were under the driving age. Today, being older, many drive, making the gang more mobile.

Weapons have become increasingly sophisticated,

making gang warfare even more dangerous. Easy avail-ability of powerful weapons has turned youth gangs into small armies.

With heavy doses of drugs often mixed into gang life, turf wars have become drug territorial wars. Turf, in some cases, means more than the place where the gang congregates. "Gangs defend their territories in order to protect their narcotic business," says Carl Taylor, in his study of Detroit gangs. "Each street corner, dope house, salesperson, distributor, or customer is part of the territory."[2] These gangs can seem more like organized crime than delinquent youth, with drug-deal shootouts fought with sophisticated artillery from speeding cars.

WHY IS GANG VIOLENCE INCREASING?

Some teenagers have few educational and job opportunities. A reputation for being tough and a good fighter is one of the only ways for these poor urban young people to attain status. An extension of the need for individual status is the need for control over territory. The gang turf may be the only area in these youngsters' lives in which they feel they have any power or control. Gang violence results from ongoing turf wars between rival gangs.

Violence has long been an integral part of the street gang's life-style. The gangs of the 1950s engaged in big fights called rumbles. Rumbles had definite arrangements and rules to be followed. Times, places, and types of weapons were agreed upon in advance by the war council or by the leaders of the two feuding gangs. The location was usually a deserted area of the city. The rumble generally took place at night, to avoid discovery by police. In those days gangs fought with fists, bats, bricks, chains, and clubs.

William B. Sanders, a sociologist, makes an interesting point about past and present gang fights, comparing them with the changing style of conflicts in our society as a whole. The huge gang rumbles involving the entire gang resembled opposing armies facing off in the large battles of World War II and Korea. The present gang-warfare style, he points out, is similar to the guerrilla warfare waged in Vietnam.

Gang fights now usually involve two or three members of a gang who ambush one or two members of a rival gang. Sometimes they seek out particular individuals. At other times they attack the rival gang in general.

The attack is usually launched to avenge or pay back a previous attack from the rivals. Frequently the attack takes the form of a drive-by shooting.

Nowadays violence is not confined to fights in deserted areas in the dark. Unfortunately it has spilled out into the daylight, affecting the quality of life of residents in urban areas and in some nonurban areas as well.

Statistics show an upsurge in the most violent crimes committed by teenagers and youth. According to the FBI, between 1983 and 1987, arrests of those under eighteen for murder jumped 23.9 percent; for aggravated assault, 19.8 percent; and for rape, 13.6 percent.[3]

By the end of 1989, in New York City, ten students had been shot, eight of them fatally.[4] On Halloween, many of the city's students stayed home because of fear of violence.[5]

Recently a new form of youth violence, called wilding, has gained national attention. The term "wilding" refers to young people cruising in a pack, roaming the streets, and violently attacking passersby for "fun." In the well-publicized 1989 Central Park jogger case in New York, a gang of teenagers, three of whom were under sixteen, went on a wilding spree. They physically and sexually assaulted a twenty-nine-year-old investment banker who was jogging—and nearly killed her.[6]

John Galea, recently retired New York City Police gang specialist, said, "The predominant group in New York City gangs now is a law-violating, disorderly group, made up ad hoc en route from neighborhood to and from school."[7]

Our society has grown more and more violent. Escalating levels of violent crimes are reported daily in the news. On television, violence not only makes the news but is often the basis of dramatic programs. By the age of sixteen, a teenager has probably watched 200,000 violent acts on television, including over 30,000 murders.[8] Slasher and horror movies as well as heavy metal music constantly pound violent messages into young people.

Child abuse plays a role in creating violence-prone teenagers, also. Some children are beaten so severely that they are left with neurological problems from head injuries that lead to violent behavior. Sexually and physically abused young people grow up angry and often turn on those around them.

Says Dorothy Otnow Lewis, professor of psychiatry at New York University, "Kids are being raised by more and more disturbed parents. And what this lack of parenting breeds is misshapen personalities."[9]

Furthermore, in some parts of the country, gang members grow up in gang-ridden neighborhoods. This "immunizes" them to the horrors of shootings and death. In fact, after some drive-by shootings, gang members have been known to refer to the innocent bystanders caught in the hail of bullets as "mushrooms."

To gang members, life is cheap.

Says Sergeant Joe Guzman of the Los Angeles Sheriff's Department Gang Unit, "Gang members think they're going to be killed anyway."[10]

Peer pressure plays a big role, too. Since status in the gang is built upon out-toughing other gangs and building up the gang's reputation for violence, violence levels inevitably increase. Since there is a state of continuing warfare, it doesn't require a specific incident for new fighting to erupt.

"Violence is inherent in gang activity," says Sergeant Bob Jackson of the Los Angeles Police Gang Unit. "A gang could be doing a car wash, and somebody could drive by and shoot at them."[11]

Hispanic gangs still fight mainly over turf, and they will defend their barrio "to the death." But they also sometimes peddle marijuana and heroin in their neighborhoods, which can add to the violence.

Twenty-nine-year-old Wizard, the leader of the Largo gang discussed in the first chapter, was killed after his followers threatened other heroin traffickers in the barrio.

Though drugs have always been a part of barrio gang life in the Southwest, the gang warfare has remained largely a neighborhood turf battle. What gave a new twist to youth gang violence was the arrival of crack cocaine in the black ghettos in the mid-1980s. Most gang members, however, do not use drugs habitually. To them, drugs are a business enterprise.

Not every gang deals drugs. Not every drug dealer is a member of a gang. But drugs are now woven into the fabric of much of the gang life, increasing the value of turf and upping the violence that goes hand in hand with turf wars.

"Drugs have been the superagents of change," says Carl S. Taylor in Dangerous Society. "Detroit urban gangs are using drugs as their vehicle for social mobility."[12]

Drug-dealing gangs have spread across the country. In some cities, local gangs have modeled themselves after those in Los Angeles. In others, branches formed when gangsters from Los Angeles moved or visited out-of-town relatives.

By 1984, Crips and Bloods from Los Angeles, already deadly street rivals, had become heavily involved with crack (or rock) cocaine. This involvement extended to the ownership of rock houses—drug operations bases. Along with the growth of the gangs' drug business came a spiraling growth of violence over territory and profits.

Crips and Bloods have appeared in Seattle, Washington; Portland, Oregon; Omaha, Nebraska; and other cities.[13] "We've had an increase in gang violence since 1988," said Lieutenant Loren Boydstun of the Denver Police Gang Unit. "We're on a direct trade route from L.A. to Denver to Omaha to Kansas City for Bloods and Crips. More people are moving from L.A. and recruiting for gangs."[14]

In the South, the Miami Boys, or Untouchables, have been pushing crack in Miami, Atlanta, Savannah, and other cities. Jamaican posse gangs have cornered the drug trade in a number of cities and have even infested a poor neighborhood in a small town in West Virginia.[15]

According to Special Agent James Watterson of the U.S. Bureau of Alcohol, Tobacco and Firearms, "The bigger crack becomes, the bigger the posses get. And what's scary is that the crack problem just keeps getting worse."[16]

People have compared gang drug dealing with Mafia bootlegging during Prohibition. But today's crimes are much more violent because of the availability of sophisticated weapons. Drug-trafficking gangs arm themselves with Uzis, AK-47 assault rifles, and AR-15 semiautomatics.

Gangs involved in drug dealing have formed branch operations and are making enormous profits by selling drugs in states where there isn't much "business competition."

For example, Minneapolis police report an influx of Bloods and Crips from Los Angeles and of Young Boys, Inc., a violent Detroit narcotic street gang. The twenty-three gang murders in Minneapolis during 1990 were drug- and turf-related, says Patrolman Mike Schoeben, police gang specialist.

"In some cases, Bloods and Crips are working together, as entrepreneurs in the drug business," he says.[17]

Albuquerque, New Mexico, a medium-sized south-western city with its share of urban poverty and troubled teenagers, has also attracted gangs. Albuquerque's Police Department recently formed a specialized gang unit to deal with the violence of drug-dealing gangs from Los Angeles.

"Sixty-five to seventy percent of the drugs in Albuquerque are gang-controlled," says Sergeant Ralph Kemp, head of the gang unit. "Violence goes up because drugs go up. Drugs are a catalyst for fighting."[18]

But Professor Irving Spergel of the University of Chicago doesn't agree that drugs are the sole reason for the increase in gang violence. "Most gang violence is not drug-related," he says. "Individuals involved in drug trafficking are mostly older and have grown out of street gangs."[19]

Former NYPD gang expert John Galea says, "Drug groups will employ those in traditional street gangs or loosely organized crews—just like working for McDonald's."[20]

Sergeant Bob Jackson of the L.A. Police Gang Unit says that "drug gangs" is a misconception. "The Crips and Bloods use individual gang members as part of their drug dealings. The more that gang members become involved in drug dealing, the less they're going to function as a street gang. It's bad for business to have kids shooting each other on the street corner because it brings the police in."[21]

Thus, as a gang member becomes more successful in drug dealing, he drifts away from street gang activity. He can still demonstrate his loyalty to the gang by providing drugs, guns, or money to the gang, but close contact with the gang is an added risk to the dealer. When the dealer forms his own drug-dealing organization, his right-hand men will usually be trusted fellow gang members. He hires his friends from the gang to work as street dealers and contract killers. It is easy to spot which of his old gang friends are working for him. They wear the regulation drug dealers' beepers to facilitate their business.

Profits from drug deals go to the person who sells the drug. The gang as a whole is not part of a cooperative drug business. But many gang fights erupt over drug turf when another gang tries to move in on the neighborhood.

Unfortunately, drug profits are a strong temptation for unemployed black and Hispanic teenagers.

Sergeant Jackson says, "How can you tell a kid who is making $500 a week guarding a rock house that he really ought to be in school or that he ought to be getting up at six o'clock every morning to walk a paper route?"[22]

A sixteen-year-old former member of a notorious gang in Detroit said in an interview in Dangerous Society: "Sure you see people with nice things and good jobs. But that's them. I'm not going to live for a long time. If a crew [gang] don't get you, something will. . . . Would you work for some $3.35 an hour when you know you can make $300 an hour? Naw, you would be rolling [selling drugs] 'cause that's the American way."[23]

Often these young people have grown up with drugs all around them in their neighborhood. The grown-ups they see every day may be using or selling drugs—or both. Sometimes it's their own parents or an older brother or sister.

In the life-and-death gang warfare of poor neighborhoods, the enemy is faceless. Most gang members don't know the names of those they are shooting at, or why they are enemies to be destroyed at all cost.

Little Ducc said he shot someone "cuz he was an enemy." Asked why the person was an enemy, he shrugged and said, "Cuz."[24]

Gang violence "is the closest thing the United States has to battle within its borders, and many of the children emerge from the streets of Los Angeles more psychologically scarred than the young mujahedin who patrol the mountain passes of Afghanistan."[25] They, too, grow up knowing only that "they"—those on the other side—are the enemy. This cycle of faceless "defend our side to the death" activities perpetuates the violence to the younger members of the fighting groups.

Some community agencies in California, New Mexico, and other states are bringing rival gangs into a neutral setting and engaging them in a joint activity, such as an employment or recreation program. The agencies hope that this will get them to see one another as people and eliminate some of the hostilities.

In the past, youth gang violence was often ignored by others because it focused only on other gangs. But now, with sophisticated transportation and weaponry and the spread of drugs, innocent people—passersby, classmates, neighbors—are being killed and injured.

Youth gang crimes that affect innocent people often attract more attention than violence between gangs. In fact, some people feel that police, city officials, and the general public do not regard gang violence as a problem *unless* it affects non–gang members. In other words, people frequently look the other way when young gang members kill each other.

Criminologist Barry Krisberg agrees with this view. In the *International Annals of Criminology* he wrote: "A Philadelphia policeman working for the gang control unit told me he really didn't care, 'as long as they killed each other—but I'm concerned about innocent bystanders.' "[26] Krisberg also reported that an elected official, commenting on a series of murders in San Francisco's Chinatown, announced to the press that "No Caucasians have been killed in Chinatown." Krisberg's point was that, for this official, the tourist trade was of more concern than the lives lost.

5

TYPES OF GANGS

Whatever the urban population mix, the newest youth gangs will be made up of people from the most recent group of immigrants. Fifty years ago Irish, Italian, and Polish gangs roamed the streets in cities where we now see black, Hispanic, and Asian gangs.

As Walter Miller, an anthropologist, has written, "The social observers of New York City in the 1880s, when the city was swarming with Irish gangs, would have been incredulous had they been told that within the century the police would be hard put to locate a single Irish gang in the five boroughs of the city."

Back then, the Irish, Italians, and Poles were the cities' poor. They were followed by Hispanic immigrants, trying to make a new life for themselves and their families in this country while fighting a language barrier, poverty, and discrimination. With the movement of many people from the rural South to the urban North, black families were soon crowded into inner-city ghettos. After the discriminatory quotas on Asian immigrants were lifted in the 1960s, waves of poor Chinese began arriving in this country, filling the Chinatowns—Chinese neighbor-hoods—in large cities.

The countries of origin of today's new immigrants—Central America and Southeast Asia—are often filled with violence. When the people arrive here, they often settle in areas that house existing street gangs—an instant introduction to new violence.

As more and more young people grow up troubled, in problem families and in poor social conditions, youth gangs are growing and spreading from one city to another. In Los Angeles, New York, Philadelphia, and Chicago, certain gangs have been around for a long time. Some gangs that originated in California have expanded into Oregon, Arizona, Utah, Texas, New Mexico, Nevada, Colorado, and Minnesota. Often, core members of Hispanic gangs who had lived in California returned to their hometowns in other states. There they have established their own gangs that imitate California street gangs in structure and activity.

All youth gangs are not alike, though they do have common characteristics—for example, they all serve as substitute families for poor ghetto youths with few educational or job opportunities and no role models. As we have noted, some youth gangs are heavily involved in drugs as a business. Others aren't. There are other differences and similarities.

MOTORCYCLE GANGS

Several old movies have featured large groups of tattooed, long-haired, violent men who upset entire towns by roaring through the peaceful streets on their Harley-Davidson motorcycles and threatening passersby. The movie characters were based on the infamous motorcycle gang, the Hell's Angels, who for many years have operated out of California. The other big motorcycle gangs are the Bandidos on the West Coast and the Pagans in the East. Motorcycle gangs still function like the big gangs of the 1950s in their formal structure of leadership. They are known for their criminal drug and gunrunning activity as well as for disrupting the life of a community. Though often portrayed as teenagers, the members of motorcycle bands are generally older.

HISPANIC GANGS

Hispanic gangs have existed in the barrios—Hispanic ghetto neighborhoods—in southern California for several generations. Often members of a family grow up in a particular gang as part of their family culture. Their father, uncles, and maybe even grandfather belonged to the gang. The family has passed down gang tradition as a symbol of their heritage and status, just as a well-off middle-class family might pass down a tradition of membership in a service club or fraternity. These ghetto families feel that their gang traditions are something to be proud of, and this becomes their legacy to the younger generation. Unfortunately this tradition guarantees yet another generation lost to street violence.

The White Fence, one of the oldest Chicano gangs in Los Angeles, was closely involved in neighborhood life centering around the church during the 1920s and 1930s. During World War II, the older members of the group left to go to war, and many did not return to the barrio. With the older members gone and with more Chicanos moving into the area, junior high school boys began fighting with long-established gangs from nearby neighborhoods. It was then—in the middle and late 1940s—that White Fence turned into a violent gang.

While some Hispanic gangs are old and well established, new ones are also springing up to fight the endless cycle of bloody turf wars.

Most Hispanic gangs have common characteristics. They do not have recognized leaders, but look to the most experienced fighter available at the moment needed. They are usually divided into cliques, or subgroups, according to age. If a new recruit does not already have a street name or nickname, he takes one when he joins the gang. The gang's name is generally related to its neighborhood. This is natural, since gang and barrio are so interconnected, and gang members consider themselves soldiers and protectors of their barrio. The name Maravilla 18th Lomas, for example, designates the region, street, and hills the gang lives in.

Hispanic graffiti is very carefully and elaborately drawn. Barrio gangs take great pride in their graffiti. They also sport plenty of "body graffiti"—that is, tattoos with the gang logo. Hispanic gangs do not generally adopt special colors. Their traditional gang uniform consists of a white T-shirt, thin belt, khaki pants with split cuffs, and a black or blue knit beanie or baseball cap with the gang logo on the visor.

BLACK GANGS

Black gangs are more individualistic and nontraditional than Hispanic gangs. They usually have only a few veteran members and a less clearly defined structure than Hispanic gangs. Black gang members are less turf-oriented and less loyal to their neighborhood. They regard themselves as Mafia-type gangsters rather than neighborhood soldiers. Black gang members are also more individualistic in dress than Hispanics, but black gangs will—as in the case of the Bloods and the Crips—identify themselves with certain colors.

Crips originated in the West Los Angeles area in the early 1970s. After the Crips grew larger and gained a strong reputation, other gangs began incorporating the word "Crip" into their gang name—such as "Kitchen Crips," "5 Deuce Crips," "Rollin' 20 Crips."

Some people think that the Crips got their name

from a gang member who had crippled legs. Others think the name came from New York gangs, where some gang neighborhoods were called cribs. Another theory is that Crip came from the movie *Tales of the Crypt*.

Another black youth gang, formed in the early 1970s in the Los Angeles area on West Piru Street in Compton, was called the Compton Piru. They soon used the term "Blood" for a gang I.D. They became stronger and, like the Crips, other gangs took the Piru-Blood name. The name Blood may have originated with the fact that young black men sometimes refer to each other as bloods.

Although the Crips and the Bloods are often cited as the two largest black gangs, they aren't really large gangs at all. They are actually small bands who add "Crip" or "Blood" to their gang name. These small groups are formed along neighborhood lines and are called sets. Often one group of Crips doesn't know the group down the street. If they meet up with them, they consider them enemies, just like any other rivals for turf. In gang life, bordering each other leads to war. Nobody cares if the enemy also has "Crip" attached to his gang name.

The Crips' greatest enemy, however, is a Blood gang and vice versa. Bloods, who call their gangs Piru, after Piru Street where they originated, don't usually fight other groups of Bloods. There is a practical reason for this: their armies can't afford the losses. Fearing extinction more than one another, they refrain from killing fellow Bloods and concentrate their energies and weaponry on their traditional rivals: Crips.

In the 1980s, some members of the Crips and Bloods became involved in drug trafficking, mainly rock, or crack, cocaine.

Crips, as we saw in Chapter 2, identify with the color blue; Bloods, red. Members of the gangs will wear red or blue bandannas, caps, belts, shoelaces, shirts, and pants. Crips and Bloods are so violently attached to these colors and what they symbolize that young people living in Crip- and Blood-infested neighborhoods carefully avoid wearing either color, so as not to provoke violence.

Crips are partial to British Knights tennis shoes. The brand's BK insignia, to them, stands for "Blood Killer." In that same vein, Bloods wear Calvin Klein jeans, as a "Crip Killer" statement. The very sight of BK tennis shoes is enough to provoke an attack by a Blood, as is the effect of CK clothing on a Crip.

Crips overwork the letter C in conversations and graffiti. Some Crips will even go so far as to substitute the C for B when talking with another Crip. The same is true for Bloods and the letter B.

Though killing each other over brands of sneakers, letters of the alphabet, and colors of clothing seems unbelievable, it is an extension of the gang member's whole existence revolving around the gang identity. If the gang stands for a person's whole sense of self, then everything he has, wears, or says is colored by gang identity. Thus, from the gang member's distorted viewpoint, any insult to even the trappings of gang identity is grounds for battle.

Though Crips and Bloods are primarily black teenagers and young adults, whites and Hispanics have been recently recruited into these gangs. Besides enlarging their pool of membership applicants, the gangs—as mentioned earlier—have spread from Los Angeles into cities such as Omaha, Nebraska; Portland, Oregon; Denver, Colorado; Minneapolis, Minnesota; and Seattle, Washington.

CHINESE GANGS

Although Chinese youth gangs are a relatively new phenomenon in the United States, their origins go back to a mystical religious group formed over three hundred years ago in China. The group, called the Triad Society, was made up of Buddhist and Taoist priests who opposed the

Manchu emperor, K'ang-hsi, who reigned from 1662 to 1722. The members of the society devoted themselves to humanitarian political causes. They escaped persecution by the emperor by going to Hong Kong, where eventually three-quarters of the population was said to be connected to the Triad.

After Sun Yat-sen founded the Chinese Republic and used the Triad organization politically, its members began fighting among themselves and turned to criminal activities. American versions of these Triad criminal groups arrived here in the nineteenth century and became known as Tongs. In the early days of Chinese immigration, the Tongs served as legal and business advisers in Chinese communities, helping newly arrived Chinese make their way among the strange customs of Western culture. But they often exacted a price from those they helped, in the form of loyalty to the Tong. Eventually, the Tongs functioned mainly as criminal organizations. Each Tong employed its own youth gang to help run gambling, extortion, prostitution, and other illegal activities. The younger boys acted as lookouts for their employers, watching out for police. These boys, as a group, were called Wah Chings. After the Tongs became more legitimate, the Wah Chings took up where the Tongs left off. The Wah Chings soon split into two factions and then split again. This led to open gang warfare among the three groups. The three gangs—Yu Li, Joe's Boys, and Wah Ching—have spread to some of the major cities in this country.

However, according to John Galea, former NYPD gang expert, "A lot of Oriental gangs are now on their own, with no ties to criminal Tong organizations."[1]

MIXED ASIAN GANGS

Today, many Asian gangs are made up of a mix of ethnic groups, since there is no longer a language barrier—the young people all speak English. For example, in Long Beach, a suburb of Los Angeles, there are a dozen mixed Asian gangs. The majority of the members are Cambodians, and there are links between California's Cambodian gangs and those in Lowell, Massachusetts; Houston, Texas; and Seattle, Washington. Two of the most notorious gangs, which are Cambodian and Laotian, are the Tiny Rascals and the Asian Boys.[2]

Some of the other gangs in the Los Angeles area are the Black Dragons, who are ethnic Chinese from Vietnam; the Oriental Lazy Boys, consisting of Vietnamese, ethnic Chinese, and Cambodian; the Ninja Clan Assassins, who are ethnic Chinese from Vietnam and Taiwanese; and the Viet Boys, made up of ethnic Chinese from Vietnam and Vietnamese.

These gangs commit home invasions, in which half a dozen heavily armed Asian gang members go into a house in their own community after they have cased it and pistol-whip, rob, and torture the residents. Asian gangs are also associated with the extortion of Asian businessmen.

An interesting twist in some of today's Asian gangs—particularly those with Cambodian members—is that they are copying Hispanic and black gang styles in dress and in flashing gang signs.[3]

VIETNAMESE GANGS

Though organized gangs have existed in urban Chinese ghettos in the United States since the 1960s, New York's Vietnamese gangs, about two years old, are much more violent than Chinese gangs, according to police sources.

Nancy Ryan, chief of Manhattan District Attorney Robert M. Morgenthau's Asian gang unit, said, "Even the other Chinese gangs say they [Vietnamese gangs] are wild and unpredictable and [they] are afraid of them."[4]

As an example of the degree of violence they are prone to, at the New Jersey funeral of a member of the Born To Kill Vietnamese gang, in July 1990, rivals opened fire on one hundred mourners.[5] The rival gang attacked with Uzi automatic weapons, leaving five wounded at the cemetery. The funeral was for twenty-one-year-old Vinh Vu, described by police as Born To Kill's number two man. Born To Kill takes its name from the slogan that some American soldiers wore on their helmets during the Vietnam War. The drug-trafficking New York gang has branches in Houston, Boston, Los Angeles, and other cities.

OTHER ASIAN GANGS

Samoan gangs, found in southern coastal areas of California, are more like black and Hispanic gangs than other Asian gangs are. They mark their turf with graffiti and wear characteristic gang clothing. Like nearly all other gangs mentioned in the book, Samoan gangs are violent, use weapons, and are involved in criminal behavior. The only exceptions are skinheads and stoners, who are only sporadically violent.

Filipino gangs are also similar in structure to Hispanic gangs and often become affiliated with them. Filipino gangs are seen mainly in San Francisco and Los Angeles, but have also appeared in cities in Alaska and Washington State.

There are two very active Korean gangs in the Los Angeles area. The strongest is the Korean Killers, who "specialize" in committing burglaries. This gang uses a Korean telephone book, published by the Korean business community, to select its burglary victims.

Their chief rival is another Korean gang, the American Burgers, who took their name from their hangout, a hamburger stand.

These two gangs use martial arts to fight each other.

Korean Killers and American Burgers join the gangs as teenagers and remain in them until they are adults.

JAMAICAN POSSE GANGS

Jamaican gangs call themselves posses, after the armed bands in American western movies. They are said to have started as neighborhood gangs in Kingston, Jamaica, that smuggled marijuana from Jamaica to the United States. Soon they graduated into crack and regular cocaine. These extremely violent groups have an estimated membership of five thousand in this country.[6] Jamaican posses have been implicated in eight hundred drug-related murders.[7] Jamaican posses are found in Miami, New York, Washington, D.C., Dallas, Houston, West Virginia, and even Anchorage, Alaska.

SKINHEADS

Skinheads originated in Great Britain as a white youth cult during the 1960s. Their appearance—boots, shaved head, tattoos—was designed to symbolize tough, angry, working-class young people. They are considered neo-Nazis because of their racial and religious bigotry. They often wear Nazi symbols and have been known to verbally and physically attack members of minority groups. According to the Anti-Defamation League of B'nai Brith, which monitors racial and religious prejudice, the number of skinheads in New Jersey is on the rise. Nationally, there are about three thousand of them in thirty-four states.[8]

STONERS

Stoners are white gangs who started out as "party" groups that eventually turned violent. They are known as stoners because of their heavy drug use. They are often involved in punk rock, heavy metal music, and Satanism.

GIRLS IN GANGS

The majority of youth gang members are male, but according to Anne Campbell, author of a book about female gang members, 10 percent of New York City gang members are girls.[9]

Today teenage girls play a stronger role in youth gangs. Some even have their own organization, though it is generally a branch of a male group.

Traditionally, girls associated with a gang have stashed drugs and carried weapons, primarily because male police would not search them. Now, however, girls will not hesitate to use the weapons in backing up their homeboys and in their own fights with other gangs.

In her book, *The Girls in the Gang*, Anne Campbell said, "Today, girls fight over boys but also fight in other arenas too: in gang feuds, against personal insults, and against police. Increasingly, they use 'male' weapons such as guns and knives."[10]

Sometimes girls instigate the fight. If a girl gang member goes out with a boy from a rival gang, there is one more reason for those groups to begin another round of violence. Or if a girl living in a Crip neighborhood has a boyfriend who is a Blood, when he visits, there will be trouble.

One "ladies auxiliary" gang in Los Angeles is the Tiny Diablas. The Diablas are connected with a local male gang, the Grape Street Watts. The thirty or so Hispanic teenage girls in this gang range in age from fourteen to nineteen.[11]

The Tiny Diablas have their own, milder version of a male initiation rite—being beaten up by veteran gang members. For the girls, it's a short punching and hair-pulling ceremony. Like their male counterparts, they take a gang or street name on joining. Girls in the Tiny Diablas collect dues from the group to buy guns, just as other groups of high school girls might collect money to buy a stereo or take a trip.

Girls from two New York City gangs, interviewed for *The Girls in the Gang*, tell why they joined:

> The Devil's Rebels (Ladies):
> " . . . 'cos once you're in a gang, you know you got your backup and leaders, and mostly all the gangs, they stick together. 'Cos if someone pushes you from another gang, they don't care, they'll fight all of them because they pushed you. . . . "
> Shadows of Death:
> " . . . Everybody grew up . . . and they noticed that . . . you don't have a friend, you don't have any friends. . . . It's like everybody's afraid of you, and they're going to be your friend and they're going to be nice to you and stuff like that because they know that you might do something to them if they don't. . . . "[12]

According to law enforcement officials, girls in gangs are more violent than they were in the past, but they are not as violent as their boyfriends are—yet.

CREWS

Some groups maintain that they are not violent street gangs. They refer to themselves as crews rather than gangs. They do, however, mark their turf with graffiti, and they engage in vandalism. In some cases, however, the word "crew" is used to mean violent gangs, as in Detroit gangs.

According to Steve Valdivia, director of Community Youth Gang Services, a program that tries to stop gang violence in Los Angeles, "These are the gangs to keep an eye on for tomorrow. Because a lot of gangs started out as crews and turned into violent gangs before long."[13]

Gangs can be directed to activities that are more positive—for themselves and for the community they live in. In a later chapter we will discuss the ways in which Community Youth Gang Services and other groups help turn gangs around.

6
GANGS IN THE MEDIA

Like other events considered newsworthy, criminal acts of youth gangs are frequently documented on television and in newspapers and magazines. Like other current events, the activities of youth gangs serve as dramatic material for movies and television programs. Featuring youth gangs in movies and television dramas is an outgrowth of our society's long-standing fascination with its own violence. Youth gangs are romanticized just as 1920s bootleggers and present-day racketeers and terrorists are.

Does the media coverage affect youth gang activity? Is it educational or harmful to publicize gangs?

On the one hand, youth gang activity is news and, as such, is considered suitable for reporting on television and in print. News stories are the method by which the public becomes informed about a social issue. In order to solve a social problem, the public needs to know that it exists, what the extent of the problem is, and the way in which it affects society.

On the other hand, publicity about youth gangs can make them attractive to young people living in gang-infested areas. The publicity enhances their reputation for violence; this, in turn, can encourage them to engage in further violence.

Furthermore, movies and dramas, in trying to create an interesting story, often romanticize gangs, distorting the truth by portraying gang members as adventure-loving outlaws, instead of dangerous, violent criminals.

One recent movie about youth gangs used actual gang members in the filming. Theaters promoted the film by handing out bandannas in gang colors with the tickets.

Colors, a 1988 movie about gang wars in Los Angeles, stars Robert Duvall and Sean Penn as gang cops trying to stem the bloody tide of violence, vengeance, and just plain viciousness. Crips and Bloods and Chicano homeboys are here in full gang regalia, up to their usual activities: emptying ammunition at one another and at passersby. The movie begins with a Blood-Crip murder in a shooting spree, progresses to shotgun blasts from cars, and ends with a Chicano gang member killing Duvall during a gang fight.

The good thing about *Colors* is that it doesn't have a happily-ever-after ending. In the end you know that though the gangsters are quiet for the moment, they'll be back doing the same things in a very short time. They aren't sitting around questioning the bloodshed, the terrible waste, or their sense of values. They aren't about to change their style or go straight.

That one element of accuracy is the good news. The bad news is that *Colors* glamorizes gang life, with its bright red and blue uniforms, wild partying, and rap song lyrics. Using real Bloods and Crips as movie extras and dispensing gang colors to hype ticket sales didn't help to solve the gang problem.

In making Bloods and Crips "movie stars" in the film and by naming the notorious gangs, *Colors* served as the Bloods' and Crips' personal publicity agent. The movie certainly gave them increased fame from coast to coast.

Did the movie promote violence?

Sergeant Ralph Kemp of the Albuquerque Police Department thinks it did. "While the movie was a factual portrayal of gang life," he says, "kids thought it made gang life glamorous. And the movie theaters' promoting the film by handing out red and blue bandannas in Los Angeles made it worse," he said.[1]

Pete Gabaldon, of Albuquerque's Youth Development, Inc., agrees. "*Colors* gave a lot of impressionable young kids the idea that joining a gang is a good thing to do. And that if you have a problem, you hurt or kill someone," he said.[2]

The Guardian Angels, the young adult civilian patrol group, protested the showing of *Colors*, claiming that the movie was a direct incitement to violence. (The Guardian Angels will be discussed in a later chapter.)

When another movie, *The Warriors*, was released in 1979, it was blamed for three killings in or near theaters where the film was playing.[3]

The Warriors deals with the trials and tribulations of a New York City youth gang, falsely accused by other gangs of killing an intergang hero in the Bronx. The Warriors end up fighting for their lives through enemy gangs' turf all the way back to their home base in Brooklyn. They win all the fights, of course, and become movie gangland heroes.

Real and mythical gangs have been the subject of movie drama for years. The 1967 film, *Hell's Angels on Wheels*, glorified the infamous criminal band's exploits in its story of a gas station attendant who becomes drawn to motorcycle gang life.

West Side Story (1961) portrayed rival ethnic gangs in New York—one Anglo, the other Puerto Rican. Romance between the sister of one gang leader and the friend of the rival gang leader led to a rumble and bloodshed.

A less serious New York ethnic gang movie was *The Wanderers* (1979). Set in the Bronx during the 1960s, it

Poverty, dysfunctional families,
and peer pressure are some
of the reasons why young
people join gangs.

Facing page: Hand signals, as well as colors,
graffiti, and body tattoos, identify gangs.

Above: A back alley filled with graffiti

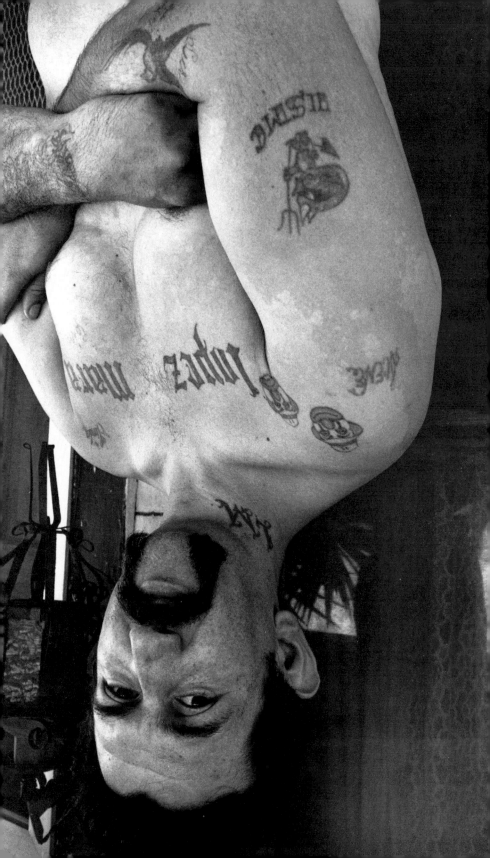

Facing page: A former gang member shows off
his tattoos. This man now works
with the California Youth Council.

Above: Gang members display hand signals.
Hand signals are a direct challenge
to other individuals and gangs.

LAST: PEREZ
FIRST: JOE
GANG: LNX 13
MONIKER: VAMP
DATE 4-27-90

JUST A FEW OF MANY

DECEASED

LENNOX AREA

GANG MEMBERS

DECEASED

A list of dead gang members on a wall of the Lennox area Los Angeles County Sheriff's Department

Lorna Hawkins, host of "Drive-By Agony," a
cable television program, holds a photograph of her
son, Joe, who was killed in a drive-by shooting.

Although the majority of gang members are boys,
teenage girls are playing a stronger role in gang life.

Above: Even a serious injury doesn't end gang life.
Here a member of a gang, confined to a wheelchair
from a gang shooting, is shown with his friends.

Facing page: Guardian Angels on patrol. Teenagers
who belong to these youth crime patrols gain
their sense of identity from helping others.

Facing page: Sergeant Joseph Guzman of Los Angeles County Sheriff Department's Operation Safe Streets, East Los Angeles office, patrols in his car.

Above: At times, girls who have a boyfriend in a gang or those who live in a neighborhood of gangs will fight right alongside the boys.

"Rest in Peace" wall dedicated to members of a gang who have died

Lieutenant Chuck Bradley, Gang Enforcement Team,
Los Angeles County Sheriff's Department, points
to a chart listing gang-related homicides.

depicted a real Bronx gang—the Fordham Baldies—and a classic full-scale rumble.

According to a Brooklyn police inspector, there can be real fallout from violent gang movies many years after they were filmed. As recently as 1982, Inspector John J. Hill commented on the effects of *City Across the River*, a 1949 movie about the Amboy Dukes, a Brooklyn gang: "Every time they play *City Across the River* again on TV, I have another homicide, a new gang fight, and three gangs change their name to the Dukes."[4]

This movie was still having an effect on teenage gangs—over thirty years after its release!

Movies and television dramas about gangs can provide real information—or misinformation—about gangs.

For example, a 1990 episode of the television show, "21 Jump Street," purported to deal with gang terrorism in a high school. In the story, a member of the Frazier Boulevard Bloods, getting revenge on the principal, took students and faculty hostage, assisted by three members of his gang.

But this supposed picture of a tough gang gave a totally unrealistic depiction of gang violence. In response to the arguments hurled by police and school administrators, the Blood's leader waved his gun in the air and said to his victims, "Only kidding." When a Jump Street officer, posing as a pizza delivery boy, angrily asked for payment, he was told to, "Shut up and eat some pizza."

A real gang member probably would have answered any argument, real or imagined, with much more violence.

A 1989 cable television drama, "Nashville Beat," gave a more realistic picture. This was a story about Los Angeles gang unit police transplanted to Nashville, where they deal with a transplanted L.A. rock cocaine gang.

"Things are getting hot for them in Los Angeles, so they've taken their merchandise on the road," said the gang expert.

"You make them sound like organized crime," said his captain.

"Pretty close," said the first. "They're just newer at it."

The gang in "Nashville Beat" is cold-blooded and vicious, like a real gang. The members aren't content simply to rob a store; they also brutally beat the owner. They then gun down a police officer and are arrested while making a drug deal with undercover police.

This type of picture doesn't whitewash, romanticize, or glamorize the gang problem, but shows it for what it is.

A December 1990 episode of "Hunter," the television police drama series, depicted one of the major causes of the perpetuation of gangs: the generational gang family. In the show, Carlos, a middle-aged Hispanic gang member, released from prison, is determined to live a law-abiding life with his family. But both his father and his son, now also a father, are heavily into the drug-dealing gang. Carlos tries to keep himself and his son away from the grandfather and the gang.

"The gang has a stranglehold on our house," says the wife of Carlos's son.

Carlos is killed in a drive-by. The gang cycle is finally broken for the next generation when Carlos's son moves away from his family-connected gang with his wife and baby.

Many law enforcement and community agency officials believe that publicity about gangs in movies, magazines, newspapers, and television shows helps increase the level of violence.

"The gang members are now part of the show," says Steve Valdivia. "It's their way of becoming a hero. And the media plays right into it by making them a star for a day, a week."[5]

After all, joining a gang is a way to compensate for a lack of success in other areas—not being able to read and write, not having a satisfactory family life, not having a future: a lot of "nots." The media attention rewards their one "successful achievement": violent behavior.

Gang members' existence and self-worth are tied into gang identity and recognition. Publicity about the gang's exploits feeds these needs.

Gang members want to be recognized by the people of their neighborhoods, and perhaps even by the public as a whole. This accounts for the defense of turf and the establishment of a reputation for violence. If a gang can inspire fear among neighbors and passersby, it has achieved a certain type of recognition, of status. Its existence is noted, even if in a negative way. The gang is talked about, worried about. Someone has noticed it.

All too often, when gang exploits are reported in the newspapers, magazines, and television, the publicity serves to incite further violence. When a gang realizes that it has gotten attention for killing someone or committing another type of violent crime, the violent behavior is, in a sense, rewarded.

Just as some teenagers keep scrapbooks of their school and athletic activities and honors, gang members often keep scrapbooks of newspaper clippings describing their gang's exploits. Sometimes, after a gang fight, rival gangsters will run home and look for details on the ten o'clock news. They'll talk about it the next day, bragging, "Did you see the news last night? We were on TV."

Not only that, but if somebody from a gang is killed and it makes the news, then the gang has an obligation to maintain its "rep" by retaliating violently enough to make the news the next night. It can be a drive-by, a kidnapping, or some other crime—as long as it's "newsworthy."

By focusing on gangs themselves instead of on the gang problem, the media can make the situation worse. Community and law enforcement groups have been working to educate television and newspaper reporters about how publicity aggravates the problem. They have asked television and newspaper reporters not to print or broadcast gang names but to refer to "rival gangs" in reporting gang-related crime and to let the gangs know that they are not going to publicize them.

Gang movies and television programs can have another kind of influence in addition to giving gangs publicity. They can help sway young people who are still in the wannabe stage. A movie or television program making gang life seem exciting and "cool" can help push a young person in that direction. On television or in a movie, often a young person sees only the colorful aspects of gangs—the uniform, the outlaw existence, the macho posturing. The blood and death aren't real and, in some cases, aren't even depicted in the story. In many instances, the gang experience looks like a magical life of adventure.

According to law enforcement and community agencies, middle-class teenagers from comfortable homes have been drawn into joining a gang because it looks "cool." They have an unrealistic view of what it's like, and by the time they realize their mistake, it's too late. They're already another gang's sworn enemy and a walking target, as are their friends, relatives, neighbors, and classmates in this no-win cycle.

Says Sergeant Kemp, "Instead of TV showing kids standing on the corner throwing their signs, show a sixteen-year-old who was mistaken for a gang member, sitting in blood in the street. That's how it really is out there."[6]

Glamorizing gang life is similar to glamorizing drug use. Teenagers who begin taking cocaine do not think of it as the start of a downward journey toward addiction, physical suffering, and illegal activities to support the all-consuming drug. When a young person first takes a drug, he or she feels it will be an exciting adventure that will not do any lasting harm. It is the same thing for outsiders who think gangs are exciting and don't know the effects on those who are in them.

Whether the results are good or bad, the media do play an educational role in publicizing gangs, because most people base their understanding of gang activity not on direct experience but on news reports. The media must maintain a balance between reporting a growing threat to society and printing or broadcasting sensational stories to increase circulation or boost ratings.

For example, the language used in a *USA Today* series on Los Angeles gangs, "The Gangs Run Wild," made pretty scary reading: "From shadowy slits off the network of freeways, where residents cower behind locked doors, to gentle boulevards where suntanned UCLA coeds stroll, it's a 24-hour life-and-death clock and gangs control the time card."[7]

And in a *Newsweek* article: "The Drug Gangs": "Bleak by day and terrifying by night, south-central Los Angeles could be set for some B-picture about the world after a nuclear apocalypse—a nightmare landscape inhabited by marauding thugs and hard-nosed cops, a world in which innocence is hostage to violence and bystanders too often wind up as victims."[8]

The task of reporting gang incidents objectively is further complicated because the problem is more prevalent in poor neighborhoods. Eventually, inner-city gang violence is no longer considered news because the crime rate has reached such heights and because of the area in which it is occurring. Yet when gang activity spreads to middle-class neighborhoods, it is not only reported but embellished, according to Sergeant Wesley McBride of the Los Angeles Sheriff's Department and Sergeant Robert Jackson of the LAPD Gang Unit.[9]

Sergeant Jackson says that gang violence is "in the papers every day and generally on TV, but not if it [occurs] in a lower socioeconomic area. If it's in our south L.A. area, pretty soon they don't care. But as soon as gang members decide to go out to Westwood or Beverly Hills or some of the other more affluent areas, now the city realizes we've got a gang problem, and it hits the news."[10]

And in New York, though white, middle-class gang crime is on the increase, according to John Galea, "It's often unreported, because it's middle-class crime."[11]

This "social class" system of reporting can increase the hopelessness urban residents feel about being able to combat the violence affecting their lives and the lives of young people drawn into gangs.

Yet the media can also be used as an educational tool to help turn around gang violence in these communities. "Drive-By Agony," the Los Angeles cable television program discussed in an earlier chapter, is one example of this. The show deals head-on with the ways in which gang life affects its many victims: relatives of murdered young people, young people who kill and are killed, and the community they live in. "Drive-By Agony" attempts to educate young people and their community leaders about positive alternatives to gang life.

"We want to make an impact on the community to let them know that it can happen to anybody," says Lorna Hawkins to her television audience. "We say to you mothers out there: 'Fight back.' "[12]

Lorna Hawkins is fighting back against gang violence through television. Other individuals and groups are fighting gangs through school programs, social agencies, and law enforcement programs.

One group that has been fighting urban crime all over the country for over ten years has turned its efforts to combatting street gangs. This group, the Guardian Angels, is made up of teenagers and young adults. The next chapter will discuss how the youthful patrol organization is battling gangs and crime.

7

THE GUARDIAN ANGELS

As the California sun disappears, the band of ghetto teenagers heads for the Hollywood streets. These avenues are rich with tourists who are flush with money and excitement, oblivious to anything but the fabled glitz and glamour here. It leaves them ripe for the pickings of pickpockets and muggers, and prey to the violence of the youth gangs that prowl the famous Hollywood streets, readying an ambush attack on people out for a slow stroll or those parked in a car.

The teenagers emerging from a run-down building on Ivar Avenue know this and are prepared. Flashing their colors—white T-shirt with a red logo and a red beret—the six teenage boys slip quietly down the hill to their night's work on Hollywood Boulevard.

But this teenage crew is not out to rob, attack, terrorize, or rip off the Hollywood tourists. The group is part of a national organization known as the Guardian Angels. Their aim is to take back the streets at night for those who live here and those who are visiting. The youthful group setting out on patrol consider themselves night watchmen of Hollywood, ready to protect the innocent from the vicious.

Sergio Terrazas, the serious-eyed patrol leader, carries the two-way radio to maintain contact with headquarters. He'll call in every ten minutes or so to give the patrol's location and report on any trouble he has spotted. If the Angels see a crime in progress, they've been trained to detain the criminal, call for police, and maintain a hold on the perpetrator until the law arrives. Unlike those they do battle against, they do not carry weapons.

Sergio scans the jam-packed boulevard as he strides purposefully ahead.

"A Hispanic gang controlled that whole block over there." He motions up the street. "The first day we were out here they were throwing bottles at us, but no one got hurt. It was pretty much bad aim," he laughs. "After the first couple of weeks we more or less cleared them out. They must have moved to some other part of Hollywood."[1]

Half of his crew tonight is from Los Angeles and half from San Diego. San Diego chapter members come up on weekends to patrol with the L.A. group. Since the Angels have now organized themselves into regional groups, they coordinate their effort where needed.

Los Angeles, with 90,000 resident gang members, appears to need the effort, especially in the Hollywood area, where tourists are considered fair game for criminal gangs. Because of this, the Ivar Hawks Neighborhood Watch invited the Guardian Angels into their community to provide residents with protection against street crime and violence.

At a corner, the patrol fans out in twos. Now the Angels are on the Pathway of the Stars, where star shapes on the sidewalks memorialize movie stars, singers, and cowboys, living and dead. They march over Jack Lemmon, Gypsy Rose Lee, and Madonna.

The crowd has grown so thick with people, the Angels can barely get down the boulevard in single file.

"There's a lot of money floating back and forth here, because they're tourists," says Sergio. "A lot of these people don't know their way around. They can be very easily conned. Their cars can be broken into. They can be taken into a side street and ripped off."

That is why, he says, Hollywood Boulevard has become such a high-crime area. Hollywood, like Times Square in New York City, also attracts runaways, who become easy prey for criminals.

At the corners, Sergio claps his hands, a signal to his patrol group. They stand still, awaiting new marching orders.

"We're trying to set an example for teenagers, as a positive alternative to joining street gangs," the twenty-one-year-old leader says.

When they give their reasons for joining and staying with the group, most of the Angels echo Sergio's statement.

Take eighteen-year-old Paul, who joined the Guardian Angels earlier this year in San Diego. "I grew up in that kind of gang neighborhood," he says. "A lot of the people I grew up with are in gangs. We've had so many drive-by shootings where I live. I've been shot twice. I still have buckshot in my back. But once you're a Guardian Angel, you see the world a lot differently."

The patrollers take silent note of the strangely costumed and made-up folks who cruise the sidewalks with them.

What did people in this town of unusual-looking people think of the Guardian Angels when they first came to Hollywood? Tourists asked the Angels to pose for pictures with them, like any other media attraction. That's Hollywood!

But when the Angels first hit Hollywood Boulevard

on their night patrols, they had some adjusting to do. They had to remind themselves that they weren't there to be tourists, gazing at stars and staring into shop windows. They were there to peer around corners and into dark spots in search of trouble.

"So many different things are going on in the city, it's hard to figure out what's going on where," Sergio said. "It's really hard to know what's going to happen because so many people come here from so many different places."

Hollywood Boulevard is surrounded by gang territory. Four blocks one way, there's the Eighteenth Street Hispanic gang. Four blocks the other way, it's the Rebels, another Hispanic gang. A Crips gang is on the other side of the boulevard.

Back home in Chicago, Sergio's neighborhood was beginning to get its share of California-style drive-by shootings. One of his friends was shot. On the way home from work, Sergio saw a poster: "Now accepting new trainees. Come in and fill out an application to fight crime."

"That was the key phrase: 'to fight crime,' " Sergio emphasizes slowly and firmly. "Because I wanted to be a cop since I was a little kid. I still do. And I said, 'Why not get out there on the streets now?' "

He felt it was good experience, like being an intern for a future career. He was also drawn to the organization because of the group's national leaders, Curtis and Lisa Sliwa. "I saw them on TV and read about them in the papers, so I knew what they were all about," he says.

As leader of the Los Angeles chapter, Sergio organizes two patrols every night. The group's relationship with the Hollywood police is friendly, they say, unlike the confrontational ones in other areas.

The Guardian Angels were founded as The Magnificent Seven by Curtis Sliwa in 1979. The group's purpose was to patrol the New York City subways to help make them safer for riders.

Inner-city teenagers were mobilized to serve as watchdogs on the streets and in the subway stations in their own neighborhoods. The Guardian Angels now have chapters all over the country. Though police and city officials in some areas still view the group with suspicion, many residents, especially senior citizens and people living in crime-infested housing projects, are glad to see the patrols and cheer them on as they file by.

While street gangs get their sense of identity from inciting violence, these youthful crime patrols get theirs from helping others, easing the minds of fearful city dwellers, and making their communities a little more livable. Thus, the young Guardian Angels, who generally live in the neighborhoods they patrol, have a healthy sense of group identity and feel like important and useful members of their community.

Some nonmembers, too, have expressed their gratitude for the efforts of these inner-city young people. A *New York Times* article recounted this experience: ". . . several Guardian Angels appeared, just like guardian angels do in storybooks. Expertly, they took over, pinned the perpetrator against a wall, held him immobilized and sent for the police to make the arrest."[2] The author, a senior citizen, had been mugged in New York.

When new rail lines were routed through gang areas of Los Angeles, the Angels got ready to place patrols in the cars, just as they had in the New York subways.

Now, on Hollywood Boulevard, they patrol the bus stops on the corners. They wait for the buses to unload and reload, scanning for any activity that seems suspicious.

Pete, a nineteen-year-old from Los Angeles, says he joined because he wanted to spend his time helping people instead of just "walking around doing nothing except working."

"I'm from a high-crime area," he said. "For me, it's a positive alternative. Doing this gives me a chance to help people feel safe walking down the street at night."

Eighteen-year-old Frank, from Huntington Park in southeast Los Angeles County, says he joined because he saw what drugs could do to people. "I wanted a way out so I wouldn't be in with that kind of people. A couple of my friends, they've been hurt through gang-related violence."

Eighteen-year-old Kris says: "On the streets in East San Diego, I was on my way to school and saw somebody get shot in the back of the head with a shotgun in a gang fight right by the high school. That wasn't a pretty sight."

At Mann's Chinese Theatre, a Hollywood landmark, Sergio uses a walkie-talkie to inform headquarters of his location, but he has no crimes to report. This seems to be a trouble-free night on the boulevard despite the noise and confusion of the milling crowds.

Seventeen-year-old Ted, from San Diego, says he's sick of looking at crime in the streets. "I grew up around here," he says. "I used to live in Oakland. There are lots of gangs in Oakland. Two friends of mine were killed through gang violence. I wanted to do something about crime and violence, and this is a good way to do it."

Eighteen-year-old Frank, from San Diego, says, "Me and a friend of mine went downtown in San Diego, where it's real busy. There were drug dealings going on right out in the open so you could see what they were selling. I thought, 'That's not right. That's not how things should be.' I saw a friend of mine who was a chapter leader. He was recruiting, and I joined up." He confides, "I liked them [the Guardian Angels] ever since I was a little kid, seeing them on the news."

The patrol trots past Marilyn Monroe's and Donald Duck's sidewalk stars.

"That's what they all want to do. They want to stay

away from drugs and gangs and do something positive, like this," says Sergio, with a proud glance at his troops. "They come from high-crime neighborhoods. Instead of hanging out in the streets, they hang out with the Guardian Angels and patrol with them."

At the next corner he claps his hands as stop and go signals.

The pedestrian traffic is so heavy on weekend nights that the boulevard is closed to cars at around ten o'clock, leaving the tourists free to stroll in the street.

"See those side streets?" Sergio asks. "The gang members wait for tourists to get out of their cars so they can rob the car and steal it, or they rob the people and then take the car."

Later, the second patrol will go down the side streets.

"But we also keep a presence on the boulevard because of purse snatchings," Sergio explains.

He sighs. "It's going to take many, many years to clean this place up. Gangs have been in these communities for over thirty years. It might take another thirty years to clean them up."

Meanwhile, the Angels are out there every night in groups of six. These young people voluntarily spend their time trying to help rid the streets of gang violence and make the inner city a better place to live in.

The street violence has affected the young patrollers, too. In June 1990 their Hollywood headquarters was broken into and robbed. Two thousand dollars' worth of equipment—mostly two-way radios and battery chargers—was stolen.

Westin Conwell, the twenty-three-year-old Southwest Coordinator, says, "These guys are putting on the red beret and the T-shirt and putting their lives on the line. You never know what's going to happen out there. We've had several Guardian Angels shot at.

"Ninety-eight percent of our Guardian Angels have been recruited [because of our] visibility," he says. "The more patrols we have out in high-profile areas, the more recruits we get in. You can join a gang, write their insignias on the walls and on your arms. But that doesn't take the effort it does to be a Guardian Angel. That takes work. The Guardian Angels have everything that a gang would have: the excitement, the fun, the brotherhood. But we're giving something back to the community."

At the Angels' headquarters, a run-down building off Hollywood Boulevard, one wall is covered with a large map showing the areas of the Southwest where the Angels have chapters. It includes cities in Arizona, Texas, New Mexico, and Nevada as well as California.

Westin, who joined the group at sixteen in San Diego, is handling calls coming in from up and down the West Coast. One of the calls is from Lisa Campos, the twenty-five-year-old chapter leader from Portland, Oregon. She signed up seven years ago with a female cousin. More and more women are joining the organization these days, she says, though they are still in the minority.

"Portland has a significant gang problem," says Lisa. "The Portland chapter works closely with the Portland Police Department to fight gang violence. We have a liaison with the department. Before we go on patrol, I call the precinct and tell them we're going to be there. The police tell us which areas to patrol in. We pick up information on patrol and turn it over to police officers."[3]

Lisa, who works in a department store, would like to tighten her liaison with the Portland Police Department. She is planning to take the police officer training examination, and if she's accepted by the Portland force as a recruit, she would like to work in a juvenile gang unit. Her years of training with the Guardian Angels have helped put her on this road, she says.

Some people think that the Guardian Angels are vigilantes. Vigilantes are people who take the law into their own hands. The term "vigilante" was used to refer to bands of men in the nineteenth-century South. They got themselves up in white robes and hoods and rode off on horseback, usually under cover of darkness, searching for blacks who had "committed crimes." Over the years, vigilantism has included citizens arming themselves to defend their homes and groups like the Ku Klux Klan, who terrorize minorities under the guise of defending law and order.

The term is now used to mean any individual or group of people who take things into their own hands and exercise authority. Bernhard Goetz is perhaps the most famous of these vigilantes. When he was attacked on a New York City subway by four young black men in 1984, Goetz, who is white, shot them.

Because of the increase in violent crime and people's fears on city streets and public transportation, there has been a trend toward vigilante justice, with more and more people carrying guns for protection. Even ministers in some poor neighborhoods have applied for gun permits or armed themselves with baseball bats because of a rash of burglaries and assaults, including the murder of a priest in Bedford-Stuyvesant, a poor neighborhood in Brooklyn, a borough of New York City.

"We're tired of people breaking into our churches," said the Reverend Mr. Charles Nesbitt, pastor of Bethesda Baptist Church in Brooklyn. "Some ministers have tried to get gun permits. . . . A lot of people have guns out here. You'd better fight back; otherwise you'll be dead."[4]

Two former candidates for governor of New York State proposed plans for arming citizens to fight crime in New York City. One advocated relaxing gun-permit rules to increase the number of residents carrying guns. The other wanted a police-trained corps of "100,000 volunteer 'vigilantes' to combat crime in the city."[5]

Police in various cities have opposed the Guardian Angels' patrols, saying that members of an unarmed voluntary citizens' group could get hurt or even killed. They maintain that the group might impede police work. Police have advocated instead neighborhood crime watch or block watch groups. These are groups of neighborhood residents who are trained by local police. They form teams that patrol their neighborhood for security and report suspicious incidents to the police.

However, some residents of high-crime areas feel that the presence of the Angels' patrols provides a sense of security. Whether the Guardian Angels are seen by police and community officials as a helpful force or not, the group continues its work and remains a positive alternative to joining gangs for inner-city young people. For young wannabes who think gangs are exciting, the Angels on patrol serve as positive role models for youths who see too few of these. They view the Angels' colors as glamorous. They see the group doing brave and dangerous deeds for the benefit of their community. Their rewards are not drug money or robbery pickings or counting the number of bullets spent in hunting down rivals. Their payback is pride in contributing to their community and feeling that they do their part to help make the streets safer.

The Guardian Angels have several things in common with a youth gang: brotherhood, colors, a logo, a sense of identity, a common purpose, the excitement of the streets. But the anti-crime patrols instill a sense of pride in the Angels. Participation in the patrols builds self-esteem, rather than perpetuating the loss of self-esteem that goes with a life of violence. Patrolling the streets is legal, not criminal.

The Guardian Angels are trying to fight youth gang violence and turn young people away from joining gangs. Other groups are also working toward both goals: ridding the community of gang violence and salvaging the lives of young people from crime and bloodshed in the streets of inner cities. The next chapter will discuss school, community, and law enforcement groups that are waging war against youth gangs.

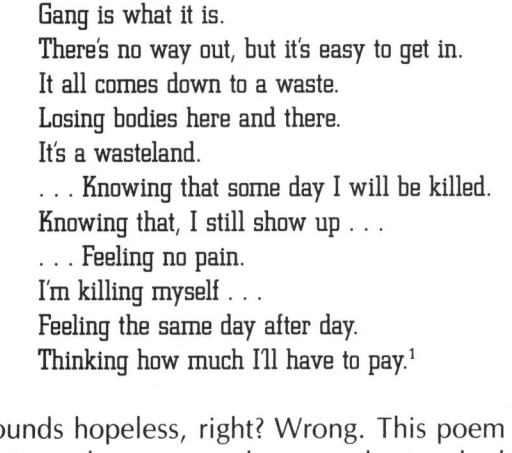

8

COUNTERATTACK

Gang is what it is.
There's no way out, but it's easy to get in.
It all comes down to a waste.
Losing bodies here and there.
It's a wasteland.
. . . Knowing that some day I will be killed.
Knowing that, I still show up . . .
. . . Feeling no pain.
I'm killing myself . . .
Feeling the same day after day.
Thinking how much I'll have to pay.[1]

Sounds hopeless, right? Wrong. This poem offers hope that youth gang members can be reached and turned away from a no-win cycle to a future with hope. The poem was written by an ex-gang member and published in a newsletter distributed by El Centro del Pueblo, a social service agency that works with gang kids in Los Angeles County.

El Centro del Pueblo is out to prove that the cycle

of gang violence can be broken. There are many other efforts being done by social agencies, community and school programs, and law enforcement agencies. Many of these groups are working together because dealing with this problem effectively requires a many-pronged approach. Ending gang violence in an area needs the efforts of the entire community.

Gangs are not only a community's problem but a part of the community itself. Like other elements of the community, they affect the lives of those living and working there.

Youth gangs affect the community's schools because gang members are school-aged and, like other young people, have made most of their social contacts in classrooms and in the school yard. Gangs affect the community's parks because parks are where young people congregate, spend their leisure time, and engage in sports.

Gangs affect the quality of life in a community. Crime committed by gangs has a deleterious effect on a neighborhood. Property is stolen or destroyed. Residents are hurt or even killed. Soon anger and fear become unwelcome residents of the neighborhood, pervading every aspect of everyday life. Violence begets further violence, as a neighborhood becomes known as crime-ridden and is given up for lost.

The splatter of graffiti on every available inch of wall space is an encroachment on neighborhood property and an intrusion into the residents' personal space and right of ownership. Graffiti-covered walls are also a visible sign, a posted notice, that a neighborhood has been taken over by a gang and that its residents have surrendered their claim to their environment.

Saddest of all is the shadow that criminal gangs cast over the future that a neighborhood's young people might have. A gang-ridden neighborhood can rob its young people of their hopes and dreams as well as twist and spoil their growing-up years. Instead of growing up healthy and whole, those children born into gang neighborhoods have had their path narrowed for them before they even learn to read.

To recap, young people in poor urban areas get involved with gangs because the gangs are an innate part of the neighborhood, culture, or family, or all three. But the gangs come into existence and flourish because the needs of the young people in a neighborhood or culture or family are not being met. The gang, in essence, fills the void.

When teenagers' needs are not met within the home, school, and society, that leads to low self-esteem and confusion of identity. The young people do not have a sense of themselves as individuals of worth. Racism and ethnic prejudice against the young people's culture from the general society further inhibits the sense of pride and self-worth in young people struggling to define themselves. They gain their self-esteem and sense of identity in the all too readily available gang culture.

The effort to reclaim a neighborhood's schools, parks, streets, and young people must involve that entire community. The police need assistance and cooperation from the area's residents to do their job effectively. Police can't begin to make inroads on a neighborhood gang problem if the residents won't get involved, won't report criminal actions, and won't help keep watch over their own community.

There are several effective methods of turning gang members around. They include programs that encourage young people to take pride in themselves and to work toward a future; programs that foster in young people the ability to see themselves as individuals, separate and distinct from the gang; programs that teach young people that they matter, are worth something, and can expect to amount to something.

If others have positive aspirations for them, young people will begin to believe in themselves. If they can view themselves as unique individuals, apart from the gang, they have the beginnings of a sense of self and of their own identity. Only then will it be possible for them to walk away from the gang. Only then will they have something to walk toward and a good enough reason to leave: themselves.

The most successful efforts in turning gang members and potential recruits around are pride-building programs for at-risk youth. Pride-building and self-esteem are at the root of most community antigang programs—because they work.

Antigang community programs that rely on local residents and services show the community caring for its own, trying to better the lives of its young people. Police officers, private citizens, city officials, social workers, parents of gang members, clergy, teachers, and gang members themselves participate in some of these worthwhile projects.

A good example of a grass-roots community worker is Chicago's Frances Sandoval, mother of a teenager murdered by gang members. She formed Mothers Against Gangs (MAG), which reaches out to teenagers in the streets to turn them away from the gangs. She tells them how their mothers will suffer if they are killed by gang violence. She tells gang members: "Get out now. Call me. I'll help you."[2]

One of the most powerful forces in the war against gang violence can be ex-gang members. Once they have grown up and changed their life-style or become worried about their own sons and daughters and their own neighborhoods, they sometimes choose to try to deter others from following their own self-destructive path.

The best time to turn young people toward a productive life-style is long before they ever start down the road of deadly violence. That means reaching out to young people as early as the third grade to get to them before the gangs do. Like programs aimed at preventing drug addiction, those aimed at preventing violence addiction need to begin early.

PROGRAMS FOR AT-RISK YOUTH

Community Youth Gang Services (CYGS) of Los Angeles is targeting third graders in its antigang efforts. CYGS staff members bring their self-esteem-based curriculum to third to sixth graders in gang-infested schools, where they teach children about alternatives to joining gangs. The fifteen-week course has a parent-teacher training program so that families and schools work together to get children interested in productive activities and away from gangs.

CYGS uses a variety of approaches in its antigang project. These include a summer youth employment service, sports and recreation programs, counseling for high-risk youth and their families, and a graffiti removal program.

Together, community residents and gang members participate in the graffiti removal program. The combination does the job and gets rid of the graffiti.

"If it is removed by neighborhood residents and neighborhood gang members, that graffiti tends to stay out. If you just clean it up yourself, it'll be up the next day, bigger than it was before," says Steve Valdivia, director of CYGS.[3]

One of the tried-and-true methods of engaging young people in healthful activity has always been sports. No matter what the participants' level of skill, sports have a universal appeal. This is no less true for teenage gang members and wannabes. Agencies working with at-risk youth are using the lure of sports as part of the slow process of redirecting gang members' addiction to criminal violence.

The method that CYGS uses is a unique variety of intergang warfare: basketball games. CYGS targets gangs that are known to be feuding. The agency hopes that once the gang members begin to interact and socialize with one another on the basketball court, they will find it a little more difficult to kill each other on the streets.

"It's head-knocking with a purpose. They're talking to each other. Maybe next time they'll talk a little more," says Steve Valdivia.[4]

Chicago's public housing authority began a midnight basketball league to help rival gangs channel their feuding into scoring basketball points. The program includes counseling for jobs, drug problems, and education. In addition to diverting young people from the streets and allowing them to work off their energy peaceably, the program emphasizes pride-building and self-esteem.

Youth Development, Inc., in Albuquerque sits members of rival gangs down together in a room. YDI staff members tell them that they don't have to like one another, but just respect each other; that they need to cool off enough to make the agency's employment program work for them. The intent of the talk sessions is to help these young people see each other as individuals, not as members of a rival gang to shoot at.

Pete Gabaldon, director of YDI, says: "This guy might have shot the other guy's brother or friend. We talk to them about respect for themselves, for other people, and for other people's property."[5]

In one unique program, YDI enlists gang members as volunteers in feeding the homeless. This is the first time anyone has expected most of these young people to help someone else. Certainly they never expected it of themselves.

Having high expectations of someone, as the YDI counselors do of these youth gang members, does a lot to raise their self-esteem. After a while, these teenagers can begin to think of themselves as people who can do something useful in the community.

Though probation departments generally work with those who have been through the criminal justice system, the Los Angeles Probation Department's GAP Program is directed at keeping young people out of the system. GAP (Gang Alternatives and Prevention) is a two-year-old program aimed at wannabes and other young people at risk for gang involvement. If a parent suspects that a young person is headed for trouble with the law, the parent can call GAP for help. Three to four hundred young people have been counseled by GAP since the program began. Says Mike Duran, director of Specialized Youth Services for the Los Angeles Probation Department, "This program is trying to keep the young person out of the system, because this is the kid that's going to end up in prison. We're talking prevention."[6]

The probation department also works very closely with young people who are tired of the gang life. "Contrary to some thinking," says Mike Duran, "a lot of these guys do change. They get tired of it or never really wanted this life-style in the beginning. Or they grow up, mentally."

Mike Duran ought to know. He's a former gang member who joined the service, came back home to the old neighborhood, and said to himself: "How can I get out? How about college?"

"And that's how I got out," he said.

ROLE MODELS

Mike Duran is a role model for the at-risk young people he deals with in the community. As a former gang member, he is living proof that there is a way out. Role models are very important for all teenagers, and particularly those at risk. The lives of young people growing up in gang neighborhoods are filled with dangerous role models: gangsters, drug pushers, addicts, and those who have given up the fight against ghetto poverty and sunk into despair. Good, law-abiding role models may help make the difference between a life of violent crime—leading to prison or death at a young age—and a future as a productive adult member of society.

Other former gang members like Mike Duran also serve as role models for young people growing up in the environment they left behind. Tony Valdez, a talk show host and reporter on KTTV-TV in California, talked about growing up gang-style: "I grew up in White Fence, the oldest gang in Los Angeles. But I learned how to read and discovered there was something beyond the barrio. Psychologically, learning to read got me out. Reading gave me imagination and other options in life.

"Now," he says, "when people like Mike Duran call on me as someone these kids could look up to, as someone who made it out of the gang life, I go, to give something back."[7]

William Celester was a teenage gang member in a poor black neighborhood in Boston. With the help of a mentor, a Massachusetts state senator, he turned his life around. Now, as a deputy superintendent of police in Boston, he's reaching out to young gang members.

Role Models, Unlimited, is a Seattle-based organization of successful community-minded black men. One of its founders is a former gang member. All have faced down overwhelming adversity to achieve their success. Their goal: to give something back to their community by serving as mentors to at-risk inner-city young black men, to prevent them from joining gangs by building pride and self-esteem.

Sometimes teenagers who have turned away from gangs want to help others headed down the same dead-end street. In Boston's ghetto areas, where over one hundred died in 1990 from gang-related violence,[8] Calvin Harris, a seventeen-year-old former gang member, is a high school junior and works as a peer counselor.

"I was in a gang," he says, "and now I'm trying to get kids out of them. But you know if you leave the gang, you've got nobody to watch your back. Plus, you still have enemies and they know where you're from. I think a lot of kids care about the shootings, but they're trying to pretend they don't care—trying to be somebody they're not," he says.[9]

SCHOOL PROGRAMS

Perhaps the most effective antigang efforts today are being carried out by elementary and secondary schools all over the country. In the past, schools taught only a strictly academic curriculum: English and other languages, math and science, social studies. Because of the drug epidemic, educators saw a pressing need to teach drug prevention in the setting most natural for learning: the classroom. The same reasoning prompted curricula in alcohol abuse, pregnancy, and teenage suicide.

To meet the need to teach gang violence prevention, the Los Angeles Sheriff's Department developed an antigang curriculum for elementary schools. It teaches children to know and value themselves as worthwhile individuals, educates them on the consequences of violence, and points out their ability to make choices. The object lesson is to foster a sense of self as a separate and distinct individual who would not have anything to gain from joining a gang and who would be able to make a conscious life choice about other alternatives.

As Albuquerque's Sergeant Ralph Kemp says: "You have to give them an identity as a kid, not a gangster. You can't just take away a kid's identity and not give him another. That's the reason he went to a gang in the first place."[10]

And, says Steve Valdivia of CYGS: "This is like a disease. In any disease, prevention is a solution. If you can inoculate someone in elementary school not to become a gang member and give him a couple of boosters in seventh and eighth grade, you've got a productive individual in society versus the costs to society of prison, people who are dead or on drugs."[11]

Ethnic awareness and cultural pride are tools that some schools are now using to "inoculate" students against gangs. A *New York Times* report announced a Milwaukee experiment: the creation of two new public schools designed for elementary and middle school black boys. The pilot program would emphasize black culture, build self-esteem, and demonstrate the rewards of responsible behavior. Though some educators see it as a type of segregation and a "special singling out of one culture," others see it as vitally necessary to help stem the tide of disenfranchised black teenage boys gravitating toward gangs and drugs, due to poverty, hopelessness, and alienation from the mainstream of the current educational system.[12]

In La Habra, a city in Orange County, California, the middle schools recently began an antigang program using Latino history for pride-building and cultural awareness, to turn young people away from gangs and motivate them to stay in school.

In a report entitled *Gangs in Schools: Breaking Up is Hard to Do*, the National School Safety Center, a clearinghouse for public safety programs, makes these suggestions for gang prevention in schools: install behavior and dress codes; constantly monitor and immediately remove graffiti; work together with parents, community groups, and law enforcement agencies to improve the self-images of gang members; and establish recreation and employment programs to assist gang members.

Above all, they state, schools must not ignore the problem of youth gangs. Ignoring gang activity does not make it go away; it only makes it worse. Redirecting gang members into the mainstream is not easy, however. It takes a strong commitment from the educational system, the parents, and the community.

The principal of Washington Prep in Los Angeles, George McKenna, says in the report: "Persons in gangs . . . need to be seen as having individual characteristics who are joined together to fulfill a personal need. The negative behavior is reflected by a group because the leadership of the group is stronger than the members, and the leadership chooses to engage in negative behavior. The members may just as easily be led by a positive force, who is stronger, and engages them in positive activity. This would therefore not make them 'chronic losers who can accomplish nothing individually,' because they could be engaged in constructive group activity."[13]

Living in a gang-infested neighborhood is difficult. But just as there are choices and a way out of a drug-filled environment, there are choices and a way out of a violent life-style. As in drug prevention, reaching out early to young people at risk for gang involvement is critical. Giving them positive alternatives, showing them that they have choices, and teaching them the consequences of a life of violence are the most effective methods of redirecting them from the gang life into the mainstream. That means getting to them before they rob a store, before they commit a drive-by shooting, before they revolt against society and are lost as productive, contributing citizens.

Our society suffers the consequences of gang violence as well as drug abuse. Communities know that they must marshal all of their resources to stem the drug epidemic. The same principle must be applied to gang violence and crime.

The long-term solution must include a full-scale attack on the root causes of youth gangs: poverty, ghettoization, racism, breakdown of the family structure, inadequate education and job opportunities, and substandard housing.

Solving social problems is never easy or quick. That doesn't mean, however, that nothing can be done in the meantime. People can and do break out of gang-infested neighborhoods and live productive, fulfilling lives. At some point along the way when they were growing up, these people developed a sense of their own worth and knew they could amount to something. Sometimes they had role models who showed them the way.

The answers to youth gangs must be:

- self-esteem and a strong sense of personal identity
- being drug-free
- the ability to resist the peer pressure of gang activity
- identification with positive role models
- education
- employment
- above all, a belief in a future

For this to happen, society must care enough to invest in its young people, for they are its future. Abandoning a new generation to violence is abandoning that future. The numbers are staggering—90,000 gang members in Los Angeles County alone. Think of what the violent actions of 90,000 young criminals could cost in lives and property. Just imagine how much good 90,000 productive young adults could do for the world.

SOURCE NOTES

Introduction
1. Interviews with members of the Los Angeles County Sheriff's Department, June 18–22, 1990.
2. Ibid.
3. Eric Harrison, " 'Murder Epidemic' Alarms Chicago," *Los Angeles Times*, June 23, 1990.
4. Mary B. W. Tabor, "In Boston, a Slaying Reawakens Gang Fears," *New York Times*, November 29, 1990.
5. Stephen J. Hedges, "When Drug Gangs Move to Nice Places," *U.S. News & World Report*, June 5, 1989.
6. Interview with Lieutenant Loren Boydstun, Denver Police Gang Unit, February 26, 1991.
7. Interview with Patrolman Mike Schoeben, Minneapolis Police gang specialist, February 27, 1991.

Chapter 1
Life in Gangland
1. All quotes from gang members are from interviews with members of Compton Barrios Largo 36, June 21, 1990.

2. Louis Sahagun, "Gang Dispute Brings Death to Party," *Los Angeles Times*, June 23, 1990.
3. Ibid.
4. Suzanne Daley with Michael Freitag, "Wrong Place at the Wrong Time: Stray Bullets Kill More Bystanders," *New York Times*, January 14, 1990.

Chapter 2
Deadly Business:
Origins, Structure,
Changes in Gangs

1. Interviews with Lieutenant Chuck Bradley, Los Angeles County Sheriff's Department, June 18–22, 1990.
2. Interview with Sergeant Ralph Kemp, Albuquerque, New Mexico, Police Department Gang Unit, June 17, 1990.
3. Susan Diesenhouse, "A Rising Tide of Violence Leaves More Youths in Jail," *New York Times*, July 8, 1990.
4. Spencer Rich, "Census Figures Find One in Five U.S. Kids Live Below Poverty Line," *Washington Post*, November 24, 1989.
5. Ibid.
6. Ibid.
7. Daniel Patrick Moynihan, "Another War—the One on Poverty—Is Over, Too," *New York Times*, July 16, 1990.
8. Carl S. Taylor, *Dangerous Society* (East Lansing: Michigan State University Press, 1990).
9. "Guns: A Day in the Death of America," Home Box Office Television, July 16, 1990.
10. Interview with Sergeant Bob Jackson, Los Angeles Police Department gang specialist, June 20, 1990.
11. Interview with Lieutenant Chuck Bradley.
12. Interview with Professor Irving Spergel, University of Chicago sociologist, February 28, 1991.

Chapter 3
Drive-By Agony

1. Interview with Lorna Hawkins, June 21, 1990.
2. Videotape, "Drive-By Agony," Continental Cablevision, Belleflower, California.
3. Interview with Sergeant Joseph Guzman, Los Angeles Sheriff's Department, June 20, 1990.
4. "The Death of a Four-year-old," *Los Angeles Times* editorial, June 23, 1990.
5. Ibid.
6. Ibid.
7. Interview with Professor Irving Spergel, February 28, 1991.
8. Interview with Patrolman Mike Schoeben, February 27, 1991.
9. Interviews with members of the Los Angeles Sheriff's Department, June 18–22, 1990.
10. Associated Press, "New Toll of Gang Shootings: Hospital to Shut Trauma Unit," February 26, 1990.
11. Eric Harrison, " 'Murder Epidemic' Alarms Chicago," *Los Angeles Times*, June 23, 1990.
12. Patricia King, "A Snitch's Tale: The Killer Gang," *Newsweek*, November 6, 1989.
13. Eric Harrison, " 'Murder Epidemic' Alarms Chicago," *Los Angeles Times*, June 23, 1990.
14. Ibid.
15. Quoted by Suzanne Daley with Michael Freitag, "Wrong Place at the Wrong Time: Stray Bullets Kill More Bystanders," *New York Times*, June 14, 1990.
16. Ibid.

Chapter 4
Violence and Drugs

1. "All Ganged Up," *Time*, June 18, 1990.
2. Carl S. Taylor, *Dangerous Society*, p.6.
3. Anastasia Toufexis, "Our Violent Kids," *Time*, June 12, 1989.

4. "Reading and Writing, Knives and Guns," *New York Times* editorial, December 9, 1989.

5. Ibid.

6. *United Press International*, "Photos of 'Wilding' Trial?" June 12, 1990.

7. Interview with John Galea, New York Police Department, retired, February 25, 1991.

8. Anastasia Toufexis, "Our Violent Kids," *Time*, June 12, 1989.

9. Ibid.

10. Interview with Sergeant Joseph Guzman, Los Angeles Sheriff's Department, June 20, 1990.

11. Interview with Sergeant Bob Jackson, Los Angeles Police Department, June 20, 1990.

12. Carl S. Taylor, *Dangerous Society*, p. 112.

13. "When Drug Gangs Move to Nice Places," *U.S. News & World Report*, June 5, 1989.

14. Interview with Lieutenant Loren Boydstun, Denver Police Department, February 26, 1991.

15. "The Drug Gangs," *Newsweek*, March 28, 1988.

16. Ibid.

17. Interview with Patrolman Mike Schoeben, Minneapolis Police Department, February 27, 1991.

18. Interview with Sergeant Ralph Kemp, Albuquerque Police Department, June 16, 1990.

19. Interview with Professor Irving Spergel, February 28, 1991.

20. Interview with John Galea, February 25, 1991.

21. Interview with Sergeant Bob Jackson, Los Angeles Police Department, June 20, 1990.

22. Interview with Sergeant Bob Jackson, June 20, 1990.

23. Carl S. Taylor, *Dangerous Society*, p. 88.

24. "All Ganged Up," *Time*, June 18, 1990.

25. Ibid.

26. Barry Krisberg, "Themes of Violence and Gang Youth," *International Annals of Criminology*, 1979–80.

Chapter 5
Types of Gangs

1. Interview with John Galea, February 25, 1991.

2. Interview with Detective Norman Sorenson, gang homicide investigations, Long Beach, California, January 10, 1992.

3. Interview with Detective Bill Park, organized crime intelligence unit, Los Angeles Police Department, January 17, 1992.

4. George James, " 'Mourners' Shoot at Least Five at Gang Member's Funeral," *New York Times*, July 29, 1990.

5. Donatella Lorch, "Mourners Returned Fire, Police Say," *New York Times*, July 30, 1990.

6. "The Drug Gangs," *Newsweek*, March 28, 1988.

7. Ibid.

8. Peter J. Sampson, "Racist Skinheads' Ranks Swell," *The Record*, June 17, 1990.

9. *The Girls in the Gang*, Anne Campbell (New York: Basil Blackwell, 1984), p. 5.

10. Ibid., p.31.

11. Seth Mydans, "Life in Girls' Gang: Colors and Bloody Noses," *New York Times*, January 29, 1990.

12. *The Girls in the Gang*, Anne Campbell, pp. 261–262.

13. Interview with Steve Valdivia, Community Youth Gang Services, Los Angeles, June 20, 1990.

Chapter 6
Gangs in the Media

1. Interview with Sergeant Ralph Kemp, June 17, 1990.

2. Interview with Pete Gabaldon, Youth Development, Inc., Albuquerque, New Mexico, June 16, 1990.

3. Vincent Canby, "When a Tame Film Inspires Violence," *New York Times*, March 4, 1979.

4. Interview with Deputy Inspector John J. Hill, 90th precinct, New York Police Department, October 1982.

5. Interview with Steve Valdivia, June 20, 1990.
6. Interview with Sergeant Ralph Kemp, June 17, 1990.
7. "The Gangs Run Wild," *USA Today*, December 8, 1989.
8. "The Drug Gangs," *Newsweek*, March 28, 1988.
9. Wesley McBride and Robert Jackson, *Understanding Street Gangs* (Placerville, California: Custom Publishing, 1986).
10. Interview with Sergeant Bob Jackson, June 20, 1990.
11. Interview with John Galea, retired, New York Police Department, February 25, 1991.
12. Videotape, "Drive-By Agony," Continental Cablevision, Belleflower, California.

Chapter 7
The Guardian Angels

1. All quotes from Guardian Angels' members are from interviews with Los Angeles–area Guardian Angels, June 22, 1990.
2. Joseph Horn, "Robbed by a Young Black," *New York Times*, May 15, 1990.
3. Interview with Lisa Campos, Portland, Oregon, Guardian Angels, June 22, 1990.
4. Howard Kurtz, "More People Are Taking Law into Their Own Hands," *Washington Post News Service*, May 16, 1990.
5. Frank Lynn, "Rinfret Seeks Volunteer Band of 'Vigilantes,' " *New York Times*, September 25, 1990.

Chapter 8
Counterattack

1. Newsletter, El Centro del Pueblo, Los Angeles.
2. "Heroes: Frances Sandoval," *People Weekly Extra*, Fall 1989.
3. Interview with Steve Valdivia, Community Youth Gang Services, June 20, 1990.

4. Videotape, "A Catalyst for Action," Community Youth Gang Services.

5. Interview with Pete Gabaldon, June 15, 1990.

6. Interview with Mike Duran, Probation Department, Los Angeles, June 21, 1990.

7. Interview with Tony Valdez, June 21, 1990.

8. Mary B. W. Tabor, "In Boston, A Slaying Reawakens Gang Fears," *New York Times*, November 29, 1990.

9. Adrian Walker, "As City's Murder Rate Soars, Fears Mount among the Young," *Boston Globe*, September 2, 1990.

10. Interview with Sergeant Ralph Kemp, Albuquerque, New Mexico, Police Department, June 17, 1990.

11. Interview with Steve Valdivia, June 20, 1990.

12. Dirk Johnson, "Milwaukee Creating Two Schools for Black Boys," *New York Times*, September 30, 1990.

13. *Gangs in Schools: Breaking Up Is Hard to Do*, National School Safety Center, Pepperdine University, Malibu, California, 1988.

BIBLIOGRAPHY

Periodicals

Associated Press. "Army Doctors Learning from Gang Warfare," November 8, 1989.

———. "Chicago Housing Agency Plans Night Basketball League for Gangs," December 2, 1989.

———. "New Toll of Gang Shootings: Hospital to Shut Trauma Unit," February 26, 1990.

———. "NY Kids Tell How Violence Changed Their Lives," November 9, 1990.

Buchalter, Gail. "Some Good Men to Look Up To," *Parade*, September 30, 1990.

Burke, David F. "Upward Bound Is Hailed by Educators," *Los Angeles Times*, June 20, 1990.

Canby, Vincent. "When a Tame Film Inspires Violence," *New York Times*, March 4, 1979.

Daley, Suzanne, with Michael Freitag. "Wrong Place at the Wrong Time: Stray Bullets Kill More Bystanders," *New York Times*, January 14, 1990.

Diesenhouse, Susan. "A Rising Tide of Violence Leaves More Youths in Jail," *New York Times*, August 1, 1990.

El Centro del Pueblo Newsletter, El Centro del Pueblo, Los Angeles.

Harrison, Eric. " 'Murder Epidemic' Alarms Chicago," *Los Angeles Times*, June 23, 1990.

Hedges, Stephen J. "When Drug Gangs Move to Nice Places," *U.S. News & World Report*, June 5, 1989.

Horn, Joseph. "Robbed by a Young Black . . .," *New York Times*, May 15, 1990.

James, George. " 'Mourners' Shoot at Least Five at Gang Member's Funeral," *New York Times*, July 29, 1990.

Johnson, Dirk. "Milwaukee Creating Two Schools for Black Boys," *New York Times*, September 30, 1990.

Johnson, Dirk. "Teen-Agers Who Won't Join When Drug Dealers Recruit," *New York Times*, January 4, 1990.

Kanfer, Stefan. "Heroes: Frances Sandoval," *People Weekly Extra*, Fall 1989.

King, Patricia. "A Snitch's Tale: The Killer Gang," *Newsweek*, November 6, 1989.

Kurtz, Howard. "More People Are Taking Law into Their Own Hands," *Washington Post* News Service, May 16, 1990.

Landers, Ann. "Our Nation's Adolescents Crying 'Help!'," *Sunday Record*, November 18, 1990.

Lorch, Donatella. "Mourners Returned Fire, Police Say," *New York Times*, July 30, 1990.

Lynn, Frank. "Rinfret Seeks Volunteer Band of Vigilantes," *New York Times*, September 25, 1990.

Moynihan, Daniel Patrick. "Another War—the One on Poverty—Is Over, Too," *New York Times*, July 16, 1990.

Mydans, Seth. "Life in Girls' Gang: Colors and Bloody Noses," *New York Times*, January 29, 1990.

Navarro, Mireya. "Shootings Jolt Children to New Views of Guns," *New York Times*, August 1, 1990.

Phillips, Christopher. "How One Problem Kid Got a Chance," *Parade*, December 2, 1990.

Rich, Spencer. "Census Figures Find One in Five U.S. Kids Live Below Poverty Line," *Washington Post* News Service, November 24, 1989.

Sahagun, Louis. "Gang Dispute Brings Death to Party," *Los Angeles Times*, June 23, 1990.

Sampson, Peter J. "Racist Skinheads' Ranks Swell," *The Record*, June 17, 1990.

Suall, Irving. "British Skinheads—Not a Passing Fad," *ADL Bulletin*, February 1991.

Tabor, Mary B. W. "In Boston, A Slaying Reawakens Gang Fears," *New York Times*, November 29, 1990.

Toufexis, Anastasia. "Our Violent Kids," *Time*, June 12, 1989.

Walker, Adrian. "As City's Murder Rate Soars, Fears Mount among the Young," *Boston Sunday Globe*, September 2, 1990.

United Press International. "Photos of 'Wilding' Trial?" June 12, 1990.

———. "The Death of a Four-Year-Old," editorial, *Los Angeles Times*, June 23, 1990.

———. "The Drug Gangs," *Newsweek*, March 28, 1988.

———. "Reading and Writing, Knives and Guns," editorial, *New York Times*, December 9, 1989.

———. "All Ganged Up," *Time*, June 18, 1990.

———. "Gunfire in L.A.," *USA Today*, December 7–8, 1989.

Books

Bresler, Fenton. *The Chinese Mafia*. Briarcliff Manor, New York: Stein and Day, 1980.

Campbell, Anne. *The Girls in the Gang*. Oxford, England: Basil Blackwell, 1984.

Fadley, Jack L., and Virginia N. Hosler. *Confrontation in Adolescence*. St. Louis: Mosby, 1979.

Foster, Herbert L. *Ribbin', Jivin', and Playing the Dozens*. Cambridge, Massachusetts: Ballinger, 1974.

Jackson, Robert K. and Wesley D. McBride. *Understanding Street Gangs*. Placerville, California: Custom Publishing, 1986.

Klein, Malcolm W. *Street Gangs and Street Workers*. Englewood Cliffs, New Jersey: Prentice-Hall, 1971.

Moore, Joan W. *Homeboys: Gangs, Drugs, and Prison in the Barrios of Los Angeles*. Philadelphia: Temple University Press, 1978.

Sanders, William B. *Juvenile Delinquency: Causes, Patterns, and Reactions*. New York: Holt, Rinehart and Winston, 1981.

Short, James F., Jr., ed. *Delinquency, Crime, and Society*. Chicago: University of Chicago Press, 1976.

Taylor, Carl S. *Dangerous Society*. East Lansing: Michigan State University Press, 1990.

Woodson, Robert L., ed. *Youth, Crime, and Urban Policy*. Washington, D.C.: American Enterprise Institute for Public Policy Research, 1981.

Yablonsky, Lewis. *The Violent Gang*. New York: Penguin, 1970.

Reports

Bowker, Lee H., Helen Shimota and Malcolm W. Klein. "Female Participation in Delinquent Gang Activities," *Adolescence*, Vol. XV, No. 59, Fall 1980.

Brown, Waln K. "An Expressive Culture Approach to Understanding Gang Delinquency," *American Journal of Correction*, July-August 1974.

Krisberg, Barry. "Themes of Violence and Gang Youth," *International Annals of Criminology*, 1979–80.

Miller, Walter B. "Violence by Youth Gangs and Youth

Groups as a Crime Problem in Major American Cities," National Institute for Juvenile Justice and Delinquency Prevention, Law Enforcement Assistance Administration, U.S. Department of Justice, 1975.

Torres, Dorothy M. "Chicano Gangs in the East L.A. Barrio," Youth Authority Quarterly, Fall 1979.

—*Black Gangs*, Los Angeles County Sheriff's Department, Operation Safe Streets.

—*Black Gangs and Narcotics and Black Gangs*, Los Angeles County Sheriff's Department, Operation Safe Streets.

—*Gangs in Schools: Breaking Up is Hard to Do*, National School Safety Center, Pepperdine University, Malibu, California, 1988.

—*Street Gangs of Los Angeles County: A White Paper*, Los Angeles County Sheriff's Department, Operation Safe Streets.

Television and Video

"A Catalyst for Action," Community Youth Gang Services, Los Angeles, California (videotape).

"Drive-By Agony," Continental Cablevision, Belleflower, California (videotape).

"Guns: A Day in the Death of America," Home Box Office Television, July 16, 1990.

Colors (movie), 1988.

The Warriors (movie), 1979.

Hell's Angels on Wheels (movie), 1967.

West Side Story (movie), 1961.

The Wanderers (movie), 1970.

City Across the River (movie), 1949.

FOR FURTHER READING

Cruz, Nicky. *Run, Baby, Run*. South Plainfield, New
    Jersey: Bridge Publishers, 1972.
Hoenig, Gary. *Reaper: The Story of a Gang Leader*.
    Indianapolis: Bobbs-Merrill, 1975.
Sale, R. T. *The Blackstone Rangers*. New York:
    Random House, 1971.
Thompson, Hunter S. *Hell's Angels: A Strange and
    Terrible Saga*. New York: Random House, 1967.
Thrasher, Frederic M. *The Gang: A Study of 1313
    Gangs in Chicago*. Chicago: University of Chicago
    Press, 1963.
Whyte, William Foote. *Street Corner Society*. Chicago:
    University of Chicago Press, 1981.

INDEX

106

107

ABOUT THE AUTHOR

Sandra Gardner is a contributing writer for the New Jersey Weekly section of the *New York Times* on youth and family issues. This is Ms. Gardner's fourth book for young adults. She lives with her family in New Jersey.

ABOUT THE PHOTOGRAPHER

Cary Herz is a corporate and editorial photographer, and a photo-correspondent for the *New York Times*. Ms. Herz lives in Albuquerque, New Mexico.